# *What*
# WORKS
# *May*
# HURT

# *What*
# WORKS
# *May*
# HURT

## SIDE EFFECTS IN EDUCATION

Yong Zhao

## TEACHERS COLLEGE PRESS

**TEACHERS COLLEGE** | COLUMBIA UNIVERSITY

NEW YORK AND LONDON

Published by Teachers College Press, 1234 Amsterdam Avenue, New York, NY 10027

Copyright © 2018 by Teachers College, Columbia University

Cover photo by Scott Rothstein via Shutterstock.

*Library of Congress Cataloging-in-Publication Data is available at loc.gov*

ISBN 978-0-8077-5905-9 (paper)
ISBN 978-0-8077-7690-2 (ebook)

Printed on acid-free paper
Manufactured in the United States of America

25  24  23  22  21  20  19  18          8  7  6  5  4  3  2  1

# Contents

# Acknowledgments

I could not have written this book without the encouragement, insights, and support of many individuals. While I am not able to acknowledge everyone who has contributed to the book, there are a number of individuals who indirectly influenced the writing of the book. David Berliner at Arizona State University gave me great insights very early on when I was just beginning to contemplate the idea of side effects. Ken Frank at Michigan State University read an early draft of the article this book is based on. Ken, as a longtime friend, colleague, and collaborator, gave me excellent feedback that greatly improved my thinking. Ron Beghetto at the University of Connecticut is another close friend and colleague I discuss ideas with, and of course he significantly influenced my thinking.

It was Dennis Shirley, professor at Boston College and editor-in-chief of the *Journal of Educational Change*, who helped me bring the idea of side effects to publication. I had put the idea of side effects into a draft of an article but set it aside for over 2 years until Dennis asked me to consider submitting it for publication in the *Journal of Educational Change*. Thanks to the efforts of Dennis and the reviewers, the article *What Works Can Hurt: Side Effects in Education* was published in early 2017.

Jean Ward, my editor at Teachers College Press, encouraged me to expand the article into a book. Although I had thought about the idea, it was Jean who put me into action. Moreover, Jean's diligence, professionalism, and wisdom greatly enhanced the book.

A group of my colleagues at the University of Kansas had a direct impact on the ideas in the book. While I was writing it, I worked with a team to develop a proposal to study side effects. Members of the team include Barbara Kerr, Mike Wehmeyer, Neal Kingston, Argun Saatcioglu, Jamie Basham, David Hansen, Sean Smith, Trina Emler, and Jasmine Padhani. Ken and Ron joined remotely as members of the group. While all of them helped me advance the idea of side effects through our weekly meetings, I owe a special thank you to Neal Kingston for bringing aptitude–treatment interaction to my attention and to Barb Kerr for broadening my views of educational outcomes.

Finally, without the support of my family, I would not have been able to devote the time to this project. More important, every one of my family members was the toughest critic of earlier drafts of the book. Their good-humored critiques made the final product much better.

While I am grateful to everyone who has affected the ideas in the book, any and all errors are my own.

—Yong Zhao, Lawrence, KS, February 9, 2018

# Introduction

"Ibuprofen may cause a severe allergic reaction," you are warned when you buy a bottle of Advil, and "this product may cause stomach bleeding." Medical products are required to disclose clearly their intended effects and known side effects. The intended effect of the common pain reliever Ibuprofen, for example, is to temporarily relieve "minor aches and pains." The drug's known side effects include allergic reaction and stomach bleeding. Hence ibuprofen products must carry a warning label about their potential adverse effects.

But it is unlikely that anyone has received such a warning about educational products.

"This program helps improve your students' reading scores, but it may make them hate reading forever." No such information is given to teachers or school leaders.

"This practice can help your child become a better student, but it may make her less creative." No parent has been given information about effects and side effects of instructional practices in schools.

"School choice may improve test scores of some students, but it can lead to the collapse of American public education." The public has not received information about the side effects of sweeping education policies.

It is also rare to find published research studies in education that report the potential adverse effects of an intervention. Educational research typically has focused exclusively on collecting evidence to prove or disprove the benefits or intended effects of products, programs, policies, and practices. The recent movement toward evidence-based educational practices and policies is only about gathering and verifying evidence for effects. It shows no concern for negative side effects.

Does this mean that educational products are immune to adverse side effects? Does it mean that all educational products have no negative impact on students?

\* \* \*

The old Chinese saying "drinking poison to quench thirst" was my first thought when the No Child Left Behind Act was enacted (No Child Left Behind Act of 2001, 2002). The law had bipartisan support and was widely viewed as the right solution to some of the most persistent problems in American education: low achievement in reading and math and the growing achievement gap. The only loud protest at the time was that it was an unfunded federal mandate, meaning that if there were more money to support its implementation, the solution prescribed in the law would really lead to transformative changes in American education.

As readers will see in Chapter 1, the main ingredients in the NCLB solution were testing and accountability, a focus on reading and math, and scientifically proven effective instructional materials and strategies. Having grown up in China, I had personal experience with testing and accountability. I knew how high-stakes testing corrupts education, turning it into test preparation. I knew how a test-driven education causes damage to the physical and psychological well-being of students, parents, and teachers. I knew that a test-driven education does not result in citizens who can defend a democracy, nor does it produce the creative and innovative individuals needed in the modern economy. I knew that it does not reduce inequity, either, and actually, as it has been practiced in China, such an education perpetuates inequality. The Chinese have struggled with the poisonous consequences of a test-driven education for a long time. I discuss this in Chapter 4.

NCLB was intended to quench the urgent thirst for better education, but the solution it proposed was wrong. It was the poisonous wine in the Chinese saying, "*yinzhenzhike*," or "drinking poisonous wine to quench thirst." The solution might appear effective in relieving thirst temporarily, but it kills in the long run. I decided to write a book to warn about the long-term damage of NCLB. The book, *Catching Up or Leading the Way: American Education in the Age of Globalization*, was published in 2009.

I was not so naïve as to think that my book would stop the self-destruction in American education, but I am happy that I sounded the warning. As it turned out, NCLB caused massive damage to American education. It did little to solve the problems as intended and forever changed the landscape and spirit of American education, for the worse. More important, the research and thinking I did for the book led me to pursue a line of inquiry that has proven meaningful for thinking about educational issues.

\* \* \*

"Medicine can be poisonous" is another Chinese saying that I found applicable to NCLB. The law claims to turn education into a field of evidence-based practices. The phrase "scientifically based research" was mentioned over 100 times in the law. It tied funding to practices that had been proven effective with scientific evidence. With billions of dollars in funding, the law pushed the evidence-based movement to new heights in education. Educational research was encouraged to learn from medicine, a field that has seen transformative changes that can only be envied by education. The primary lesson to be learned from medicine was randomized controlled trials (RCT). But NCLB neglected to take into account another valuable lesson that helped transform medicine into modern medicine: Medicine can be poisonous.

The backers of NCLB and other advocates of evidence-based practices were interested only in proving the effectiveness of interventions—that is, whether or to what degree an intervention causes the intended outcome to happen. They did not consider the side effects—secondary adverse effects—of the interventions. But my observations of education in China and the United States suggest that education, just like medicine, can have side effects, causing harm while doing good. The Chinese education system, on the one hand, is very effective in producing a compliant and homogenous citizenry and workforce, but it has failed to produce creative and diverse thinkers. The U.S. education system, on the other hand, seems to be able to cultivate more creative entrepreneurial individuals but fails to teach the basics to a large group of children. Does this suggest that certain educational practices can be effective in achieving certain goals but can hamper the realization of other, equally important goals?

\* \* \*

This question led me to explore side effects in education. Side effects in education can happen for a number of common-sense reasons. First, time is a constant. When you spend time on one task, you cannot spend that same time on another. When a child is given extra instruction in reading, he or she cannot spend the same time on art or music. When a school focuses on only two or three subjects, its students do not have the time to learn something else. When a school system focuses on only a few subjects such as reading and math, students won't have time to do other and perhaps more important things.

Second, resources are limited. When they are put into one activity, they cannot be spent on other activities. When school resources are devoted to the Common Core, other subjects become peripheral. When schools are forced to focus only on raising test scores, activities that may promote students' long-term growth are sidelined.

Third, some educational outcomes can be inherently contradictory. It is difficult for an education system that wishes to cultivate a homogenous workforce to also expect a diverse population of individuals who are creative and entrepreneurial. Research also has shown that test scores and knowledge acquisition can come at the expense of curiosity and confidence.

Fourth, the same products may work differently for different individuals, and in different contexts. Some people are allergic to penicillin. Some drugs have negative consequences when taken with alcohol. Likewise, some practices, such as direct instruction, may work better for knowledge transmission, but not for long-term exploration. Charter schools may favor those who have a choice (can make a choice) at the expense of those who are not able to take advantage of the choice.

This book is about my discoveries over a decade. Briefly, I have discovered that any educational intervention, for the obvious, common-sense reasons mentioned above, can do harm. I also have found that ignoring side effects is one of the main reasons for the perpetual wars and pendulum swings in education. Furthermore, I found that neglecting side effects has led to the dismissal of interventions that actually may be effective in some contexts. Overall, neglecting side effects has hindered the progress of education.

The specific focus of each of the chapters of the book is as follows: Chapter 1 discusses the negative side effects of No Child Left Behind. Chapter 2 uses evidence of the side effects of the Reading First program to discuss why simply borrowing randomized controlled trials from medicine does not lead to educational transformation. Chapter 3 follows the long-fought battle about the effectiveness of direct instruction and uncovers some of the negative side effects of direct instruction in general and of Direct Instruction in particular. Chapter 4 discusses the effects and side effects of East Asian education systems, pointing out that high performance on international tests comes at the price of student well-being and creativity. Chapter 5 uses visible learning to illustrate one major source of side effects: multiple and sometimes competing educational outcomes. Chapter 6 uses teacher qualifications and school vouchers as examples of another major source of side effects: individual variation. Chapter 7 discusses the consequences of not attending to side effects, with examples of the reading and math wars as well as the perpetual pendulum swings of educational ideas. Chapter 8, the final chapter, is a call to action for policymakers, researchers, and consumers of education. It illustrates how attending to side effects can help education move beyond century-old wars such as child-centered versus curriculum-centered approaches. The chapter concludes the book with specific recommendations for policymakers, educational researchers, product developers, and education consumers (i.e., parents, teachers, and school leaders).

I intend this book to serve a number of purposes. First, it is a call to policymakers and education leaders to begin paying attention to potential adverse effects when they develop and adopt policies and programs. Instead of looking only at evidence of effectiveness, they should ask for evidence of potential side effects in order to make informed decisions. Second, this book is a challenge to educational researchers and intervention developers. They should study both effects and side effects and disclose them to consumers. Studying side effects also can incentivize them to continually refine their interventions. Third, I hope this book can stimulate interest in providing information about side effects in education to consumers, potentially in the form of a consumer's guide for teachers, parents, and students. While I am able to present evidence of side effects of some interventions in this book as examples, I have not been able to gather such evidence for many other, more popular interventions. I am hoping that this book can raise awareness of side effects among consumers of educational products—programs, policies, teaching strategies, curriculum, educational technology products, and so on—so that they will demand such information when making and accepting choices.

\* \* \*

American education faces many uncertainties today. But one thing is certain: We will see a slew of new policy proposals as states implement the Every Student Succeeds Act and whatever actions the new administration may take, in addition to the mind-boggling number of products, programs, and services already vying for the attention (and money) of parents, schools, and education systems. When making decisions about policies and products, we should ask for information about their adverse effects in addition to evidence of positive effects.

What works can hurt!

# CHAPTER 1

# When Risks Outweigh Benefits
## The Effectiveness, Effects, and Side Effects of NCLB

"This is a good bill for the American children," pronounced President George W. Bush in January 2002 at the signing ceremony of the No Child Left Behind Act. Surrounded by supporters and leaders from both political parties, he promised that the bill would usher in "a new era, a new time in public education in our country." As a result, he declared: "From this day forward, all students will have a better chance to learn, to excel, and to live out their dreams" (Bush, 2002).

The new era in American public education promised by President Bush has come and gone. As intended, it was a tumultuous era, an era marked by massive disruptions and changes at all levels of education from classrooms to state and federal governments. The changes touched everyone in education and beyond—students, teachers, school administrators, school board members, state officials, textbook publishers, testing companies, and even the general public. NCLB so drastically changed American education that Thomas Dee, University of Virginia professor of public policy and economics, and Brian Jacob, policy and economics professor at the University of Michigan (2010), believe it to be "arguably the most far reaching education policy initiative in the United States over the last four decades" (p. 149).

The changes prescribed by NCLB did not result in its intended effects. Instead, a host of adverse side effects ensued. The side effects generally have been considered unintended consequences; indeed, they were not intended, but perhaps they could have been prevented had we studied side effects of educational interventions. If Congress and the Bush administration had the knowledge of the damages caused by NCLB that we have today, they could, or should, at least have given the law a second thought.

### THE DIAGNOSIS AND PRESCRIPTION

NCLB was designed to treat the illness of the achievement gap that has plagued America and American education for a long time (Harris &

Herrington, 2006; Hess, 2011; Hess & Rotherham, 2007; Ladson-Billings, 2006; Paige & Whitty, 2010; Reardon, 2011; U.S. Department of Education, 2002a; Zhao, 2016b). Although views differ as to whether the term *achievement gap* adequately captures the problem (Jones, 2013; Ladson-Billings, 2006, 2007; Royal, 2012), it has become a household catchphrase to describe the persistent chasm in educational achievement between children from advantaged backgrounds and their counterparts from disadvantaged backgrounds. Through no fault of their own, some children are much less likely than others to have a high level of educational achievement.

## Symptoms

The symptoms of the achievement gap include the historical pattern of differences in math and reading scores between students of different ethnic backgrounds and family income (The Annie E. Casey Foundation, 2010, 2013; M. J. Bailey & Dynaski, 2011; Duncan & Murnane, 2011; Ford & Grantham, 2003; Fryer & Levitt, 2004; Plucker, Burroughs, & Song, 2010; Plucker, Hardesty, & Burroughs, 2013; Reardon, 2011). For example, the National Assessment of Educational Progress (NAEP) consistently has found that Black and Hispanic students score significantly lower than their White counterparts (National Center for Education Statistics, 2012). This disparity is found also in other forms of standardized tests such as the SAT, the test used by many colleges in the United States for admission decisions. An analysis by the Brookings Institute found that in 2015 "the average scores for blacks (428) and Latinos (457)" were "significantly below those of whites (534) and Asians (598)" (Reeves & Halikias, 2017). Similar gaps exist in high school graduation rates and school dropout rates (National Center for Education Statistics, 2017), as well as in college attendance and graduation rates (Ginder, Kelly-Reid, & Mann, 2017).

> *The achievement gap is one of the most significant social issues in America. . . . Closing the gap is thus both a moral and an economic mandate.*

The achievement gap is one of the most significant social issues in America. It is a matter of social justice and an issue of civil rights (Ladson-Billings, 2006; Paige & Whitty, 2010). It is morally unacceptable and antithetical to the American ideal of equal opportunity for all (Arrow, Bowles, & Durlauf, 2000; Darling-Hammond, 2010; Ladson-Billings, 2006). Furthermore, it is an economic issue because the achievement gap has serious social and economic consequences (The Annie E. Casey Foundation, 2010, 2013; Darling-Hammond, 2010; Espenshade & Radford, 2009; Jencks & Phillips, 1998; McKinsey & Company, 2009; Plucker et al., 2010;

Plucker et al., 2013). Closing the gap is thus both a moral and an economic mandate. It is an effort whose purpose is to both remove inequality in education and increase economic prosperity and competitiveness.

## Diagnosis of Causes

There are different diagnoses of the illness. The causes of the achievement gap are complex and complicated (Hess & Petrilli, 2004). Social and economic inequality has been identified as one of the main causes (Berliner, 2006; Koreman & Winship, 2000). Children living in poverty, regardless of their race and ethnicity, perform worse than their wealthier counterparts (Crane, 1996; Tate, 1997). The history of racism and racial segregation is another major cause (Jones, 2013; Ladson-Billings, 2006; Valencia, 2012, 2015). And of course, schools are another significant contributor. The schools that poor and minority children attend are much more poorly resourced and more environmentally challenging than the schools of their wealthier suburban counterparts (Darling-Hammond, 2010; Valencia, 2015).

While all the diagnoses are valid, NCLB took a narrow and simplistic view of the causes. It pointed to schools as the primary cause of the achievement gap. To be more precise, NCLB identified the people who work in schools, not the material resources and social and cultural capital, as the main cause. According to the diagnosis of NCLB, the achievement gap was the result of teachers and school leaders. Lower-performing schools were staffed with less qualified teachers and administrators, who also had lower expectations of their students and taught them with unscientific methods, than higher-performing schools. Moreover, these teachers and administrators might not have wanted to work as hard as others to improve their students' achievement.

> NCLB identified the people who work in schools, not the material resources and social and cultural capital, as the main cause.

## The NCLB Prescription

Following the diagnosis, NCLB offered its prescription for treating the illness of the achievement gap. There were four major ingredients that targeted the perceived causes of the condition. The first was test-based accountability (No Child Left Behind Act, 2002). "First principle [of NCLB] is accountability," said Bush (2002). "In return for federal dollars, we are asking states to design accountability systems to show parents and teachers whether or not children can read and write and add and subtract in grades three through eight." The law required states to test math and reading of all elementary school children and publish the test results so that schools and teachers could be held accountable. This ingredient was ostensibly to address the belief that teachers did not want to improve their students' achievement.

The accountability measures prescribed in NCLB went beyond testing and publication of testing results. To address the achievement gap problem, the law required states to disaggregate test results for different subgroups according to student characteristics such as race/ethnicity, English proficiency, disabilities (special education), migrant status, and poverty (free and reduced-price lunch). Schools had to show that they were making adequate yearly progress (AYP) for each subgroup in standardized math and reading scores. Otherwise they faced sanctions including staff reconstitution with the possibility of replacing the principal and staff, closing and reopening as charter schools, being taken over by the state, or being subjected to other major governance restructuring.

The second ingredient was school choice (No Child Left Behind Act, 2002). NCLB allowed parents to choose other public schools or use free private tutoring if their child attended a school deemed needing improvement. "Any school that doesn't perform, any school that cannot catch up and do its job, a parent will have these options—a better public school, a tutor, or a charter school," said Bush at the 2002 signing ceremony. "We do not want children trapped in schools that will not change and will not teach." The school choice measure was intended to increase parental choice and, more important, to add pressure to public schools.

The third ingredient was the so-called scientifically based programs (No Child Left Behind Act, 2002). As discussed elsewhere in this book, NCLB devoted large amounts of resources to identifying and disseminating scientifically proven effective instructional models and strategies. The Reading First program, discussed in Chapter 2, exemplified this spirit of NCLB. As Bush (2002) explained:

> [W]e're going to spend more money, more resources, but they'll be directed at methods that work. Not feel-good methods, not sound-good methods, but methods that actually work. Particularly when it comes to reading . . . we've spent billions of dollars with lousy results. So now it's time to spend billions of dollars and get good results.

The fourth ingredient was "highly qualified teachers." NCLB requires states to put "a highly qualified teacher" before every student in every classroom. A "highly qualified teacher" must have a bachelor's degree and full licensure or certification, and prove that he or she knows the subject he or she teaches. States must measure the extent to which all students, particularly minority and disadvantaged students, have highly qualified teachers. States also must adopt goals and plans to ensure that all teachers are highly qualified and must publicly report their plans and progress in meeting teacher quality goals (No Child Left Behind Act, 2002). This ingredient targeted the perceived problem of low-quality teachers in low-performing schools.

In addition, NCLB significantly increased federal education spending and tied federal funds to accountability measures. The law won bipartisan support in Congress because it addressed issues of concern to both sides of the aisle. When it was first signed, the law also enjoyed enthusiastic support from the general public (Loveless, 2006b). For example, the 34th annual Phi Delta Kappa/Gallup Poll released in September 2002 found that 67% said they supported annual testing of students in grades 3 to 8 to track students' progress, one of the main components of NCLB (Rose & Gallup, 2002).

## THE EFFECTS AND EFFECTIVENESS OF NCLB

"It's 2014. All children are supposed to be proficient. What happened?" asked NPR's lead education blogger Anya Kamenetz (2014), checking in on one of the most important goals of NCLB, which was to have all students achieve high academic standards by attaining proficiency in reading and math by the 2013–2014 school year (No Child Left Behind Act, 2002). Actually, one did not have to wait until 2014 to know it was an impossible goal. In 2002, shortly after the bill was signed into law, assessment expert and professor at the University of Colorado Robert Linn and his colleagues (Linn, Baker, & Betebenner, 2002) pointed out the infeasibility of meeting the goal if states adopted reasonably ambitious tests and performance standards.

The point made by Linn and colleagues is critical to understanding the extent to which the goal was met, because NCLB left each state to determine the definition of "being proficient." One state could, for example, decide that being able to recognize all 26 letters at grade 3 was being proficient in reading. Thus, it could devise a test to assess children's ability to recognize the 26 letters. It then could establish 50 out of 100 points as the cut score. Accordingly, if a student got half or more of the items correct, he or she could be deemed proficient in reading. Hence, unless the standards are high, the tests rigorous, and the cut scores reasonable, it is fairly easy to achieve proficiency. Given the frequently reported cases of states lowering their standards and cut scores and the varying definitions of being proficient in the NCLB era (Kamenetz, 2014; Nichols & Berliner, 2007), the most reliable measure of proficiency is NAEP, the Nation's Report Card. Judging from the 2015 results (NAEP, 2015), the goal was far from being met.

As shown in Figure 1.1, the percentage of all students at or above proficient in NAEP reading in 2015 was 36% for 4th grade, 34% for 8th grade, and 37% for 12th grade. Math results, depicted in Figure 1.2, were not much better, with 40% of students in 4th grade at or above proficient, 33% in 8th grade, and 25% in 12th grade. The percentage of 4th- and 8th-graders at or above proficient in math and reading in 2015, a year after the NCLB deadline, was far from the stated goal of 100%, not even for the highest-performing subgroup, Asian students.

The gap between racial/ethnic groups remained significant in 2015, as shown in Figures 1.1 and 1.2. Black 4th-graders were 28 percentage points below their White counterparts in reading and 32 percentage points below in math. The difference in percentage points between Black and White 8th-graders was 28 points in reading and 30 points in math. In 12th grade, the difference between Black and *More than half of all children have been left behind.* White students in reading was 29 points and in math, 25 points. Similar differences exist between Hispanic and White students and Native American and White, as well as Hawaiian/Pacific Islanders and White. The only exception is the Asian subgroup, which consistently has shown better results than other ethnic groups, as they did in 2015.

The results were about the same in 2013 (NAEP, 2015) and in fact in all previous rounds of NAEP. Judging from the low percentage of students

**Figure 1.1. Percentage of Students at or Above Proficient in 2015 NAEP Reading**

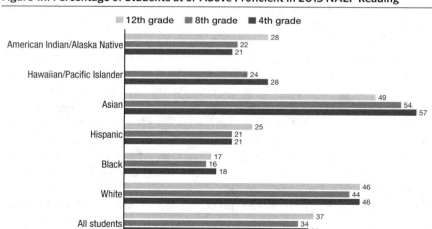

**Figure 1.2. Percentage of Students at or Above Proficient in 2015 NAEP Math**

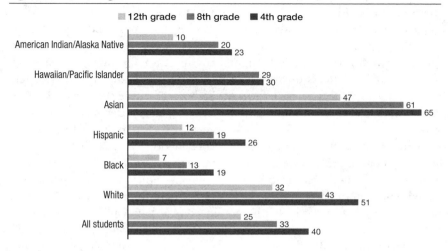

at or above proficient in NAEP math and reading in 4th, 8th, and 12th grades, the promise to leave no child behind was not realized. More than half of all children have been left behind. Judging from the big gaps between Black students and White students, Hispanic students and White students, and Native American students and White students, the achievement gap remains. It continues to plague America.

Of course, all students achieving proficiency can be viewed as political rhetoric. After all, politicians cannot propose a policy that says that only a certain percentage of students will be proficient. Even if the number was 99%, they would be challenged to answer which 1% would not be proficient. For this reason, it may be unfair to deem NCLB an ineffective treatment for failing to reach 100% proficiency.

A more reasonable and fair approach may be to assess the degree to which NCLB was effective in accomplishing its intended effects. Since NCLB was not a randomized controlled experiment but a sweeping policy, it is impossible to reach any indisputable conclusion of causality. With that in mind, scholars have employed sophisticated methods to examine the impact of NCLB on improving math and reading.

Thomas Dee and Brian Jacob (2010, 2011) conducted the most influential high-quality studies that found evidence in favor of NCLB's effectiveness. In an attempt to detect the causal effects of NCLB, they took advantage of the fact that some states had implemented accountability systems prior to NCLB and others had not. Thus, they treated the states that had introduced their own accountability systems as the control group and those that had not as the experimental group treated by NCLB. They tested for changes in the trend of NAEP scores using interrupted time series models.

Dee and Jacob concluded that NCLB resulted in a moderate but statistically significant increase in test scores in math for 4th-graders and a moderate but not statistically significant increase for 8th-graders. They did not find any effects on reading scores for either grade. The researchers also found that effects were largest at the bottom of the score distribution. Additionally, they found moderately large positive effects for 4th-grade Black students in math and positive effects for Hispanic and low-income students in both 4th and 8th grades (Dee & Jacob, 2010, 2011).

Helen Ladd, professor emeritus of public policy at Duke University, challenged these findings. She argues that the positive effect may have been overstated based on the fact that the largest gains were found in 4th-grade math in 2003, only a year after NCLB was signed into law. Ladd (2017) believes the gains cannot be attributed to NCLB: "Given the challenges of implementing a new program and the fact that education is a cumulative process, with outcomes in Grade 4 dependent in part on prior year achievement, any gains [sic] in 2003 seems far too early to attribute to NCLB" (p. 463). When the 2003 scores are removed, the effect for 4th-grade math becomes statistically insignificant.

Moreover, Ladd challenges the attribution of the slow growth of NAEP scores in the post-NCLB era. NAEP math scores for 4th- and 8th-graders improved after the introduction of NCLB, but the trend stopped in 2015. NAEP reading scores declined in the few years immediately after the introduction of NCLB and rose later. But "these trends provide little or no support for the hypothesis that NCLB raised test scores," argues Ladd (2017). She asserts that the increases were a continuation of "the upward trend that had begun in the 1990s" (p. 462).

NCLB also had other goals. But by and large, these goals were not accomplished, either. Despite the increase in high school graduation rates, the overall graduation rate was 81% in the 2012–2013 school year, far from its stated goal that all students would graduate from high school. White students still graduated at a much higher rate than Black, Hispanic, and Native American students. Low-income students, students with limited English proficiency, and students with disabilities still graduated at a much lower rate than the national average (Bidwell, 2015).

It is reasonable to conclude that NCLB was not effective in delivering its intended student outcomes. There is no solid evidence that it improved reading or math. There is no evidence that it closed the achievement gap. There is no convincing evidence that it caused the increase in graduation rates.

## SIDE EFFECTS OF NCLB

While the combination of test-based accountability, school choice, high-quality teachers, and scientifically based practices of NCLB did not effectively deliver the intended outcomes, it did have significant effects, significant effects that negatively affected millions of children and teachers as well as American public education. The negative side effects fall into four broad categories: students, teachers, schools, and culture. But again, because of the lack of attention to side effects in education policymaking and research, we do not have indisputable proof that NCLB caused these damages. However, the evidence accumulated over the decade-long period of NCLB does strongly support that NCLB resulted in the negative effects. Some of the effects actually were intended by NCLB.

### Side Effects on Students: Denial of a Real Education

NCLB was supposed to provide a high-quality education to all children, but instead it resulted in a much worse education experience for all children, particularly for disadvantaged children. Because the law narrowly defined education as reading and math instruction, it led to a significant narrowing and distortion of students' educational experiences. The narrowing came in multiple forms: reallocation of time (curriculum narrowing), teaching to the test, depriving some students of learning (discriminating attention), increased anxiety, and lost opportunities.

*NCLB . . . resulted in a much worse education experience . . . particularly for disadvantaged children.*

*Curriculum Narrowing.* It has been widely observed that the law's virtually exclusive focus on reading and math, through funding and test-based accountability, led to significant reduction of time and resources to other subjects and educational activities (Dee & Jacob, 2010; Jennings & Rentner, 2006; Ladd, 2017; McMurrer, 2007; Tienken & Zhao, 2013). With increased emphasis on improving test results in literacy and numeracy, schools had to devote more instructional time to math and reading. But time is a constant. So increasing time for reading meant reducing time for other subjects. As a result, reducing time for non-tested subjects became a common practice. The time shifting was much more significant for schools serving disadvantaged students than for those serving more advantaged children (Tienken & Zhao, 2013).

Jack Jennings, president of the Center on Education Policy, a Washington, DC-based think tank that followed the implementation of NCLB, wrote with colleague Diane Rentner (2006) about the reallocation of time to reading and math:

> To find additional time for reading and math, the two subjects that are required to be tested under NCLB and that matter for accountability purposes, 71% of districts are reducing time spent on other subjects in elementary schools—at least to some degree. The subject most affected is social studies, while physical education is least affected. In addition, 60% of districts require a specific amount of time for reading in elementary schools. Ninety-seven percent of high-poverty districts have this requirement, compared to 55%–59% of districts with lower levels of poverty. (pp. 110–111)

Devoting more time to math and reading seemed to be an intended effect of NCLB. So, in a sense, test-based accountability was effective in changing school practices. But this change in practice did not result in the intended outcome of improvement in reading and math. Instead it undermined "the potential for schools to promote other valued capacities, such as those for democratic competence or personal fulfillment" (Ladd, 2017). It also could deprive students of the opportunity to explore their interests and passions, and to find schools relevant, resulting in increased disengagement with schools. This could be especially damaging to disadvantaged students, who do not have as many home and community resources as their wealthier counterparts to afford the breadth of experiences and exposure to other subjects outside schools.

**Teaching to the Test.** NCLB was very effective in turning teaching into test preparation (Ravitch, 2013). It not only pressured schools to take time out of other subjects to prepare for tests in reading and math, but also pressured schools and teachers to focus only on content and skills within the domains of math and reading (Ginsberg & Kingston, 2014; Jennings & Bearak, 2014; Reback, Rockoff, & Schwartz, 2010). In other words, students did not even have the opportunity to experience the broader, perhaps more important, aspects of math and reading. Moreover, NCLB pressured schools and teachers not only to teach to the test, but also to teach the test by devoting time to teaching children how to take the tests. "Evidence of teaching to the test emerges from the differences in student test scores on the specific high stakes tests used by states as part of their accountability systems, and test scores on the NAEP, which is not subject to this problem" (Ladd, 2017).

Teaching to the test occurred more often for disadvantaged children. For example, a study found that programs for English language learners focused more on test content and strategies (Menken, 2006). Columbia University economics professor Randall Reback and colleagues examined the impact of NCLB on school services and student outcomes using longitudinal data. They found that teachers spent more time on test preparation in schools

> *NCLB was very effective in turning teaching into test preparation.*

that faced greater short-term pressure to meet NCLB mandates, typically schools with more disadvantaged students. But these test preparation strategies did not positively or negatively affect outcomes (Reback et al., 2010).

*Discriminating Attention.* NCLB was also effective in directing teachers' attention to certain students. Research found that, due to the accountability pressure, teachers narrowed the groups of students they attended to, focusing only on groups that were most likely to help the class meet AYP requirements (Ladd & Lauen, 2010; Neal & Schanzenbach, 2010). Schools, too, were incentivized to focus educational resources on marginal students rather than those on the ends of the ability distribution (Krieg, 2008). As a result, both high-achieving and low-achieving students were neglected. This happened more often in schools that were in danger of NCLB sanctions.

There were even worse forms of discriminating attention. There were numerous reports that some schools actively pushed out students who might be at risk of not scoring well on the mandated tests (Nichols & Berliner, 2007). Those authors found "considerable evidence that some educators have shaped the test-taking pool in their schools or districts through such extraordinary practices as withdrawing students from attendance rolls. Others have purposefully demoralized students, causing them to give up" (p. 57). For example, Lorenzo Garcia, former superintendent of El Paso schools, kept almost half of students eligible for 10th grade from taking the 10th-grade exam by not allowing them to enroll in the schools, retaining them at 9th grade, or rushing them into 11th grade (Sanchez, 2013). As a result, "high-stakes testing creates conditions in which a great number of our most vulnerable and less advantaged students are denied a chance at a productive life" (Nichols & Berliner, 2007, p. 57).

*Increased Anxiety.* Another negative side effect of NCLB was the increase in emotional stress and anxiety among students. A 5th-grade special education student explained how NCLB causes stress and anxiety, in the *Washington Post* in 2011:

Testing creates significant stress for students, teachers and parents. No Child Left Behind takes the stress of testing and assumes that the more students are prepared for testing the less anxious they will be. But what this actually does is lead students to believe that this test is far more important to their future than it actually is, since teachers, principals and parents are all busy trying to help a student for a test that will judge them. Now the student feels as if they will let all these people down if they don't do well on the test and eventually this stress for everybody leads to the student becoming so emotional and anxious that they don't even have the ability to function properly for the test that they have been worrying about. (Strauss, 2011)

The 5th-grader's observation and explanation have been confirmed by scholarly research (Cizek & Burg, 2006). A team of researchers at Michigan State University empirically studied the effects of NCLB testing on students' emotions. They found that students had significantly more overall test anxiety in relation to NCLB high-stakes testing versus classroom testing. They also found that students experienced significantly more cognitive and physiological symptoms of test anxiety in relation to high-stakes testing (Segool, Carlson, Goforth, Von Der Embse, & Barterian, 2013). This study clearly demonstrated that students experience heightened anxiety in response to NCLB testing.

> Researchers found that students had significantly more overall test anxiety in relation to NCLB high-stakes testing versus classroom testing.

***Opportunity Cost.*** Another side effect of NCLB on students was the loss of possible better alternatives. That is, students could have experienced something better than NCLB. Since their reading and math did not improve anyway, there could well be more effective interventions. Moreover, millions of children who went through school under NCLB lost their chance for a better education—the right one that might have helped them. NCLB was akin to the wrong medication applied to a patient. Its ineffectiveness caused damage and thus an adverse side effect.

### Side Effects on Educators: Changes Without Impact

NCLB has affected educators significantly, resulting in a host of changes. But these changes did not result in positive gains for students. Some of the changes have been positive for teachers. For example, a study found that NCLB led to an increase in teacher compensation (Dee & Jacob, 2010). Some other changes may have been burdensome to teachers. For instance, NCLB seemed to have led to an increase of the number of teachers with master's degrees. Obtaining a master's degree requires investment, so it would be reasonable to assume it imposed a burden on teachers (Dee & Jacob, 2010). Teachers also have reported increased pressure and working longer hours post-NCLB (Reback et al., 2011). Collaborating with peers decreased post-NCLB, but teachers reported more support from administrators (Grissom, Nicholson-Crotty, & Harrington, 2014). The degree to which NCLB affected job satisfaction has been a topic of debate. While anecdotal evidence and media reports revealed a high level of feeling pressured and less job security and satisfaction, empirical examination of national data suggested little effect on teacher job satisfaction (Grissom et al., 2014).

*Millions of children . . . under NCLB lost their chance for a better education.*

But there is one piece of evidence that warrants particular consideration. NCLB placed teachers "in untenable positions, environments where pressures encourage questionable behavior" (Nichols & Berliner, 2007, p. 34). The prevalence of various forms of cheating on standardized testing is one of those behaviors. Numerous instances of cheating by school administrators and teachers have been reported in recent years (Toppo, Amos, Gillum, & Upton, 2011), including the infamous case in the Atlanta public schools (Vogell, 2011; Zhao, 2014). The exact magnitude of the problem is difficult to quantify, but some surveys found that about 10% of teachers and administrators admitted to some form of cheating or assisting their students to obtain better results (Nichols & Berliner, 2007).

*About 10% of teachers and administrators admitted to some form of cheating.*

## Side Effects on American Educational Culture

NCLB also has caused long-term damages to education in America. These damages were done to institutional arrangements, educational beliefs, and cultural values. As a result, these damages did not end when NCLB was replaced. They will continue to affect American education for a long time to come.

*Narrow View of Purposes of Education and Schooling.* NCLB promoted an extremely narrow view of education by mandating schools to focus only on math and reading. In fact, the focus was not even on math and reading; rather, it was on raising test scores in math and reading, particularly for low-achieving, disadvantaged students. This view led to the devaluing of other subjects, and, more important, of the whole purpose of education and schooling (Hess,

2011; Ladd, 2017; Ravitch, 2013), which anyone would believe should be broader than taking tests that measure basic skills in reading and math (Dewey, 1975; Labaree, 1997). This view has already shortchanged millions of students (Hess, 2011), which is bad enough, but its long-term damage is much worse. Because of 12 years of NCLB mandates and billions of federal dollars, this narrow view of education has been drilled into the American psyche about education. Even though people do not necessarily subscribe to this narrow view, scores in reading and math often are equated with the quality of education in the media, school reports, and the collective conscious in America. The new federal education law, the Every Student Succeeds Act (ESSA), perpetuates this view of education. It is likely to affect how Americans make education decisions in policy and practice for a long time to come.

*Obsession with Testing and Standards.* NCLB's reliance on high-stakes testing for accountability has led to an increased obsession with testing and standards. America saw a dramatic increase in the time and money spent on testing in schools. It also has seen the consequences of high-stakes testing (Nichols & Berliner, 2007). There is also mounting evidence that test-based accountability does not lead to education improvement (Hout & Elliott, 2011). However, American policymakers continue to be obsessed with standardized testing. The law that replaced NCLB still mandates almost the same levels of testing in schools, for example.

> The law that replaced NCLB still mandates almost the same levels of testing.

*Rise of Charter Schools and Privatization.* NCLB has further fueled the expansion of charter schools and strengthened the push for school choice. It mandated school closures for failing to meet AYP and allowed school choice. Both measures enabled the marketization of American public schools (Ravitch, 2013).

"NCLB has contributed to widespread school closings across the country because it required schools to be ranked by test scores," said Stanford University professor Linda Darling-Hammond at a 2015 congressional forum on the impact of school closures on students and communities. Darling-Hammond argued that closing public schools has had a negative impact on student performance. It also has created hardship for communities already struggling with disinvestment. Moreover, "school closings are not isolated incidents but rather a movement toward privatization," said Judith Browne-Dianis, co-director of Advancement Project, a civil rights organization, at the same forum (Rosales, 2015). "Had the law been followed to the letter, almost every public school by now would be closed or handed over to private management," writes education historian Diane Ravitch (2015), former assistant secretary of education in the George W. Bush administration.

Ravitch was one of the strongest supporters of the test-based accountability agenda. After seeing the damage NCLB had done to public schools, she changed her views about testing (Ravitch, 2010) and began to expose "the hoax of the privatization movement and the danger to America's public schools" (Ravitch, 2013). Privatization has not reduced the achievement gap, nor has it improved the overall quality of education in America, according to Ravitch. But the end of NCLB did not end the push for privatization, as evidenced by the Trump administration's aggressive push for vouchers (McLaren & Brown, 2017).

> *Closing public schools... also has created hardship for communities already struggling with disinvestment.*

***Stifling Innovation.*** NCLB also has stifled educational innovations (Hess, 2011). With its focus on scientifically based evidence, the law looked for and supported approaches and practices that worked in the past for the narrowest of outcomes, test scores, without considering side effects. As a result, NCLB did not invest in, but rather actively discouraged, research and development of educational interventions aimed at achieving other important educational outcomes, such as citizenship. It completely ignored human abilities that have become a necessity for the future world, such as global competency, creativity, and entrepreneurial thinking (Wagner, 2008, 2012; Zhao, 2012b).

Because of NCLB, American education lost more than a decade of opportunities for innovations. The first decade of the 21st century saw breathtaking transformation in other fields, such as information technology, transportation, medicine, and agriculture. Yet American education stood still, frozen in the past. The lack of innovation will cost America dearly in the future.

## SUMMARY

In summary, NCLB was a total disaster. It was not effective for its intended outcomes, even in its narrowest definition: narrowing the gap in test scores in reading and math between disadvantaged children and their more advantaged counterparts. But it was extremely effective in causing unwanted outcomes that adversely affected students, educators, and educational institutions and culture. These side effects will take many years to undo, if they can be undone at all. Frederick Hess of the American Enterprise Institute wrote in *National Affairs* in 2011 about the damage:

> The truth is that achievement-gap mania has led to education policy that has shortchanged many children. It has narrowed the scope of schooling. It has hollowed out public support for school reform. It has stifled educational innovation. It has distorted the way we approach educational choice, accountability, and reform.

The answer to why the law was not effective in achieving its intended outcome is fairly simple: Its diagnosis of the cause of the achievement gap was wrong. The gap was more a result of poverty, segregation, racism, and lack of investment in education for the disadvantaged, instead of unqualified educators who were considered unwilling and unable to teach children well. A wrong diagnosis led to ineffective treatment.

One positive outcome that came at very high cost is that we now know that test-based accountability does not work and empirical studies of interventions without considering side effects can be disastrous. We also know that policies can have wide-ranging and long-lasting side effects. But whether we can take advantage of the costly outcome and learn the lesson for the future is uncertain. In passing the Every Student Succeeds Act (2015), Congress and President Obama seemed to still believe in the same treatment prescribed by NCLB and that it would bring better education to American children.

*NCLB ... was extremely effective in causing unwanted outcomes that adversely affected students, educators, and educational institutions and culture.*

At the signing ceremony, President Obama (2015) recognized the problems of NCLB: "It [NCLB] didn't always consider the specific needs of each community. It led to too much testing during classroom time. It often forced schools and school districts into cookie-cutter reforms that didn't always produce the kinds of results that we wanted to see." But he did not fully appreciate the severity of these consequences, nor did he consider them side effects, an inherent quality of the measures that NCLB employed for its intended outcomes. As a result, President Obama endorsed the NCLB's prescription: "The goals of No Child Left Behind, the predecessor of this law, were the right ones: High standards. Accountability. Closing the

*A wrong diagnosis led to ineffective treatment.*

*Without seriously considering the side effects of NCLB ... Obama will be proven a liar, as was George Bush.*

achievement gap. Making sure that every child was learning, not just some."
Thus, with confidence, Obama promised in 2015, as Bush did in 2002:

> Our schools will have higher expectations. We believe every child can learn.
> Our schools will have greater resources to help meet those goals. Parents will
> have more information about the schools, and more say in how their children
> are educated. From this day forward, all students will have a better chance to
> learn, to excel, and to live out their dreams.

Without seriously considering the side effects of NCLB, the ESSA undoubtedly will have results similar to those of NCLB. So, in a few years, Obama
will be proven a liar, as was George Bush, because his claim that "all students
will have a better chance to learn, to excel, and to live out their dreams" will
be proven false.

# CHAPTER 2

# The Missed Lesson from Medical Research for Education

## Why Randomized Controlled Trials (RCT) Couldn't Cure Reading First

"If ever there was a program that was rooted in research and science and fact, this is it. This is [like] the cure for cancer," said Margaret Spellings in March 2008 at a conference (Manzo, 2008a). The then-U.S. Secretary of Education was talking about the federal Reading First initiative, a cornerstone of NCLB (No Child Left Behind Act, 2002). The program provided about $1 billion each year between 2002 and 2008 to support states and districts to "apply scientifically based reading research—and the proven instructional and assessment tools consistent with this research—to ensure that all children learn to read well by the end of third grade" (U.S. Department of Education, 2002b).

But Spellings quickly was proven wrong. A month later, her own department released a report that essentially made her a liar. The interim report of a 5-year, $35 million impact study mandated by Congress found: "On average, across the 18 participating sites, estimated impacts on student reading comprehension test scores were not statistically significant" (Gamse, Bloom, Kemple, & Jacob, 2008, p. ix). "There was no statistically significant impact on reading comprehension scores in grades one, two or three," confirmed Grover J. "Russ" Whitehurst, director of the Institute of Education Sciences (Glod, 2008). The finding was reaffirmed in the study's final report released in November 2008: "Reading First did not produce a statistically significant impact on student reading comprehension test scores in grades one, two or three" (Gamse, Jacob, Horst, Boulay, & Unlu, 2008, p. xv).

### THE CASE OF READING FIRST

Reading First did not cure the cancer of low reading achievement as Spellings expected. But it would be a mistake to doubt the sincerity of her belief. She was genuinely convinced, as were many other political leaders, including legislators from both sides of the aisle in Congress and President Bush, that the program was based on solid scientifically proven evidence. At the time, the Bush administration was resolved to bring education out of the Dark Ages and transform it into a field based on scientific evidence (U.S. Department of Education, 2002c). The phrase "scientifically based research" appeared 110 times in No Child Left Behind.

> A 5-year, $35 million impact study found . . . "no statistically significant impact on reading comprehension scores in grades one, two or three."

## Science of Reading

Reading was believed to be the only area in which "we have a substantial and persuasive research base," according to Whitehurst, then-assistant secretary for research and improvement of the Department of Education. That "substantial and persuasive research base" was brought to Bush by "some of the country's leading cognitive scientists and reading researchers, including Reid Lyon, Louisa Moats, Barbara Foorman, and Claude Goldenberg" (Stern, 2008, p. 9) at a meeting on January 12, 2001, the day after his inauguration. Besides the President, first lady Laura Bush and Margaret Spellings (then Margaret LaMontagne), Bush's domestic policy advisor, were present at the meeting,

> Reading First did not cure the cancer of low reading achievement as Spellings expected.

according to Sol Stern, author of *Too Good to Last: The True Story of Reading First* (2008), a report in defense of Reading First sponsored by the Thomas B. Fordham Institute, a conservative think tank.

Apparently, these scientists successfully sold Bush their version of the science of teaching reading, which was produced by the congressionally convened National Reading Panel. The Panel was convened in 1999 to "evaluate existing research and evidence to find the best ways of teaching children to read" (National Institute of Child Health and Human Development [NICHD], 2000a). The 14-member Panel "considered roughly 100,000 reading studies published since 1966, and another 10,000 published before that time. From this pool, the Panel selected several hundred studies for its review and analysis" (NICHD, 2000a). The Panel presented its version of the science of reading in its report *Teaching Children to Read: An Evidence-Based Assessment of the Scientific Research Literature on Reading and Its Implications for Reading Instruction* (NICHD, 2000c). Since Congress was already on board, this version of reading science easily made it into No Child Left Behind and became the essential elements of Reading First (Stern, 2008).

The version of the science of reading underpinning Reading First is that reading requires explicit instruction. The Panel believed that its analysis of the research clearly showed that "the best approach to teaching reading is one that incorporates: explicit instruction in phonemic awareness, systematic phonics instruction, methods to improve fluency, and ways to enhance comprehension." Thus, Reading First required all schools and teachers to adopt reading curricula and materials that focus on the five essential components of reading instruction as defined in the Reading First program: (1) phonemic awareness, (2) phonics, (3) vocabulary, (4) fluency, and (5) comprehension.

Spellings, Bush, and all supporters of Reading First believed it to be a cure rooted in science and facts. But why didn't the cure work?

## Corruption and Implementation

For one thing, there was the outright charge of corruption. "Five years later, an accumulating mound of evidence from reports, interviews and program documents suggests that Reading First has had little to do with science or rigor," wrote *Washington Post* journalist Michael Grunwald in 2006. "Instead, the billions have gone to what is effectively a pilot project for untested programs with friends in high places." In his article "A Textbook Case: Billions for an Inside Game on Reading," Grunwald details the scandal that ultimately led to the resignation and reassignment of top officials overseeing Reading First at the Department of Education for favoritism and conflicts of interest. "Department officials and a small group of influential contractors have strong-armed states and local districts into adopting a small group of unproved textbooks and reading programs with almost no peer-reviewed research behind them" (Grunwald, 2006). "The program is being manipulated and ripped off by the people who are running the program," said then-House Appropriations Committee Chairman David Obey (D-WI) in an interview on NPR in 2007 (Abramson, 2007). In a 2007 congressional hearing, Congressman George Miller (D-CA), chairman of the Committee on Education and Labor, referred to the operation of Reading First as a "criminal enterprise" ("Mismanagement and Conflicts of Interest in the Reading First Program," 2007).

There were, of course, countercharges. Advocates of Reading First saw the corruption scandal as backlash against them. They believed it was engineered by those who stood on the other side of the reading war—the whole-language camp—and the anti-Bush liberal media. "Aggrieved vendors of whole language programs complained bitterly that their wares couldn't be purchased with Reading First funds," writes Sol Stern. "They found a receptive ear in the Department of Education's Office of the Inspector General (OIG), a bastion of green eyeshade and Dragnet types who weren't the least bit knowledgeable about the ins-and outs of reading instruction or the intent of the Reading First program" (Stern, 2008, pp. 5–6).

Advocates of Reading First celebrated Christopher Doherty, director of Reading First, who resigned after the scandal came to light, as a hero instead of a villain. Doherty, Stern's book suggests, was sacked because he was trying simply to "ensure that Reading First schools used only programs proven to work and shunned those that don't" (Stern, 2008, p. 5). The task was made harder because Congress bowed to the pressure of "commercial textbook publishers, whole language advocates and others" and eased the eligibility criteria. Instead of maintaining the strict criterion that the funds could be used only for reading curricula whose effectiveness had been validated by scientific studies, as originally envisioned by Bush, Spellings, and reading czar Reid Lyon, Congress made it possible for programs "based on" scientific research to qualify for funding too. "That opened the door to the possibility that all manner of nonsense might get funded—as it had under the Clinton-era Reading Excellence Act—unless executive branch officials held the line and hewed to the program's intentions" (Stern, 2008, p. 5).

The Thomas B. Fordham Institute's defense came out a month before the interim report of the congressionally mandated study (Gamse, Bloom, et al., 2008), which was one of "the largest and most rigorous undertaken by the U.S. Department of Education" (Manzo, 2008b). So the picture painted in the Fordham book was very positive. And we cannot know whether the author would have had a different take after seeing the results of the study showing no significant impact. The defenders' alternative interpretation of the scandal does not change the fact of conflict of interests and mismanagement (N. E. Bailey, 2013; Manzo, 2007; Office of Inpector General, 2006), but the corruption did not seem to have significantly affected the implementation of the program in terms of promoting instruction that focused on the five essential elements demanded by Reading First. The government impact study of the program found that:

- Reading First produced a positive and statistically significant impact on amount of instructional time spent on the five essential components of reading instruction promoted by the program (phonemic awareness, phonics, vocabulary, fluency, and comprehension) in grades one and two. The impact was equivalent to an effect size of 0.33 standard deviations in grade one and 0.46 standard deviations in grade two.

- Reading First produced positive and statistically significant impacts on multiple practices that are promoted by the program, including professional development in scientifically based reading instruction (SBRI), support from full-time reading coaches, amount of reading instruction, and supports available for struggling readers. (Gamse, Jacob, et al., 2008, p. xv)

These findings essentially suggest that the science of reading promoted in Reading First was faithfully implemented. So implementation was not the reason for the lack of significant impact of Reading First on reading comprehension. The issue is with the science or lack thereof behind the program.

### Biased "Science"

Advocates for Reading First repeatedly have touted the program as based on scientific evidence. But the science, distilled by 15 individuals, has been challenged as biased because not all perspectives on reading were represented on the Panel. The Panel was sponsored by the Child Development and Behavior Branch within the National Institutes of Health. By no accident, the branch chief at the time was Reid Lyon, a staunch believer in phonics instruction and George Bush's reading czar for Texas. A majority of the members of the Panel apparently had a preconceived perspective on what constitute effective approaches to teaching reading. A member of the Panel, Dr. Joanne Yatvin (2000), wrote a dissenting minority view criticizing the work of the Panel:

> From the beginning, the Panel chose to conceptualize and review the field narrowly, in accordance with the philosophical orientation and the research interests of the majority of its members. At its first meeting in the spring of 1998, the Panel quickly decided to examine research in three areas: alphabetics, comprehension, and fluency, thereby excluding any inquiry into the fields of language and literature.

As a result, the Panel excluded other important areas of research such as reading motivation, interest, and reading and writing (Coles, 2003). "The report completely ignores the areas of oral language development and motivation, presumably because there was not sufficient experimental research in those areas," according to the National Education Association (NEA, 2011).

NEA's presumption was correct. The Panel had a predetermined perspective on what counts as scientific evidence. It made clear that:

The highest standard of evidence for such a claim is the experimental study, in which it is shown that treatment can make such changes and effect such outcomes. Sometimes when it is not feasible to do a randomized experiment, a quasi-experimental study is conducted. This type of study provides a standard of evidence that, while not as high, is acceptable, depending on the study design. (NICHD, 2000b, pp. 1–7)

Correlational or descriptive research could be considered in cases when randomized experimental studies and quasi-experimental studies were too few or too narrowly cast, or of marginal quality. But no claim could be determined on the basis of descriptive or correlational research alone (NICHD, 2000b). As a result, the 100,000-plus studies were reduced to about 500 by eliminating studies that were not experimental and quantitative (Coles, 2003).

The science behind the Reading First program was apparently biased. It was selectively distilled to favor one predetermined view. But the National Reading Panel and advocates of the approach prescribed in Reading First would argue that they were working on moving education into a scientific field by insisting on randomized experiment as the gold standard of research. They believed the reason that education had not made as much progress as other fields, such as technology and medicine, was the lack of rigorous scientific method. The U.S. Department of Education (2002c) painted a dark picture of education, in contrast to the shining image of progress in other fields, in its 2002–2007 Strategic Plan:

> *The Panel excluded . . . important areas of research such as reading motivation, interest, . . . reading and writing . . . [and] oral language development.*

Unlike medicine, agriculture and industrial production, the field of education operates largely on the basis of ideology and professional consensus. As such, it is subject to fads and is incapable of the cumulative progress that follows from the application of the scientific method and from the systematic collection and use of objective information in policy making.

Ironically, as it has turned out, agriculture and industry also failed to take side effects into account, with serious consequences for public and environmental health.

To move education out of its sorry state, the touted solution was randomized clinical trials, which were assumed to have contributed significantly to the transformation of medicine. Bob Slavin (2002), one of the most vocal advocates of evidence-based education, asserts that "it is the randomized clinical trial—more than any single medical breakthrough—that transformed medicine" (p. 16).

The contribution of randomized, controlled clinical trials to the progress in medicine cannot be overstated, but it is only part of the story. RCT is a tool to ensure the quality of evidence, to make sure that the evidence is unbiased, valid, reliable, replicable, and generalizable. RCT can help to ensure the quality of evidence of effectiveness of a treatment, but it does not decide the outcome of the treatment. The human body is a complex organic living system. A treatment thus can affect one part of the system positively while causing damage to other parts of the system. Human beings also differ on an individual basis. As a result, a treatment can cure a disease for some but cause dangerous allergic reactions in others. People's situations also vary. Consequently, a treatment that works positively in one situation may cause harm in another. Modern medicine has always taken a systemic view of the effects of medical interventions, using RCT to collect evidence of effects on a variety of outcomes. It is up to the researchers to examine the effects on different outcomes and weigh the risks and benefits of the treatment.

> A treatment . . . can affect one part of the system positively while causing damage to other parts of the system.

But the National Reading Panel and proponents of Reading First looked only at the evidence of effects on a very narrow list of outcomes, while excluding others, such as reading interest, motivation, and reading and writing (Coles, 2003). It also operated under the assumption that if verified by randomized experiments or quasi-experiments, an intervention applied to all people, under all conditions, without any potential damages. This mindset—attending to only a narrow set of outcomes and expecting an intervention to work equally well for all students—is prevalent in education. It explains why Reading First failed to show evidence of significant impact on reading comprehension.

> The National Reading Panel and proponents of Reading First looked only at the evidence of effects on a very narrow list of outcomes.

## The Effectiveness of Reading First: A Speculation

When we apply a different mindset, the Reading First results provide surprising insights for the future of education and educational research. The results from the impact study (Gamse, Bloom, et al., 2008; Gamse, Jacob, et al., 2008) can be completely reinterpreted to show that the program was more than just a waste of money and time. It was effective and was not, worked and did not, as well as benefited and caused harm. However, because the $35 million study did not apply this mindset in the data collection and analysis, all interpretations are speculative.

*It Cured Cancer, But Not for All.* Reading First may have been extremely effective for some children but not for all children who participated in the program. The results demonstrate large variations across sites and grades in terms of impact on reading comprehension scores, "from reductions of nearly 30 scaled score points to increases of more than 35 scaled score points" (Gamse, Jacob, et al., 2008, p. 38). This suggests that Reading First had very positive impacts on students in some sites and very negative impacts on students in other sites. It did not have much impact on some students. But the study did not attempt to look carefully at why the program helped some, caused damage to some, and made no difference to others. Instead, applying the old mindset, it concluded that "formal tests indicated that this site-to-site variation was not statistically significant for either outcome, either by grade or overall, for classroom reading instruction or student reading comprehension, and therefore do not support the hypothesis that there is systematic variation site-to-site" (Gamse, Jacob, et al., 2008, p. 38).

*It Reduced Fever, But Resulted in Stomach Bleeding.* Reading First was shown to have had a statistically significant positive impact on decoding skills for 1st-graders, but no significant impact on comprehension (Gamse, Jacob, et al., 2008). Could Reading First be just like the cold medicine that reduces fever but can cause stomach bleeding, producing some benefits while causing other damages? It is possible that emphasis on decoding resulted in a loss of interest in reading for some students, making it plausible to hypothesize that too much time was devoted to decoding and not enough to reading comprehension, resulting in a lack of impact on comprehension for all students. But since reading interest and motivation were not included as outcomes, there is no way to confirm or reject these reasonable hypotheses.

*It Helped to Eliminate Typhus and Malaria, But Poisoned Wildlife and the Environment.* In some ways, Reading First, due to its biased science, was like DDT, which helped to eradicate typhus and malaria by killing the insects that spread the diseases in many countries and regions, but also poisoned other, beneficial wildlife and the environment. Reading First helped to spread the recommendations of the National Reading Panel, which led to the widespread use of curricula and instructional approaches aligned with explicit instruction and a focus on phonics. The Panel "has had a major impact on what has been taught and tested in reading instruction in the early grades" (National Education Association, 2011). It is not an exaggeration to say that Reading First has changed the environment of early reading (J. S. Kim, 2008). The change is not entirely positive, however, although it produced some benefits, as suggested by the trends in reading achievement between 1992 and 2015. The National Assessment of Educational Progress (NAEP, 2015) found that 4th-graders' national average reading score increased by 10 points since 2000, the year the National Reading Panel released its report. This gain could be attributed to the changes brought about by Reading First and the Reading Panel. But during the same period, 8th-graders' reading scores remained virtually unchanged (NAEP, 2015), and scores for 12th-graders actually decreased slightly from 1998 to 2015 (NAEP, 2015). Keep in mind that the 8th-graders and 12th-graders tested in 2015 may have been exposed to Reading First–inspired instruction. Can this be the consequence of an environment poisoned by Reading First, which might have delivered some benefits for early readers but actually resulted in damages later? We may never know, but we can speculate.

## Learning from Reading First

There are many important lessons we can draw from the Reading First experiment. First, randomized experiment is a technical contribution. As a method of gathering evidence, it alone does not advance education as a science. It has to work in tandem with a different philosophy. Second, the different philosophy is that there are many worthy outcomes in education and there are different students. Thus, when looking for evidence of effectiveness of educational interventions, we must take a holistic and long-term perspective. We should look not only at the effects on intended outcomes, but also at the impact on other outcomes. We should look at the effects not only on all students, but also on individuals in different situations. This is the lesson we should learn from medicine, but that has been missed in the current movement to transform education into an evidence-based field.

# SIDE EFFECTS: THE MISSED LESSON FROM MEDICINE

Today we are able to take drugs with knowledge of their effects and potential risks, and consider information about potential benefits and dangers of an operation before a decision is made. We also can go into a pharmacy and buy drugs without worrying about being poisoned. We also are told to avoid alcohol when taking certain medicine. These all resulted from the transformative progress made in medicine over the past few decades. This progress owes a lot to two major pharmaceutical disasters and lessons learned from them.

## The Elixir Sulfanilamide Disaster

"The first death was that of two-year-old Robert 'Bobbie' Sumner, who succumbed at his aunt's home on Thursday, September 30th 1937. . . . The day after Bobbie Sumner died, an 11-month-old girl and eight-year-old boy expired," writes Barbara Martin in *Elixir: The American Tragedy of a Deadly Drug* (2014, p. 2). The book documents the tragic death of more than 100 Americans, many of them children, caused by the very medicine prescribed to cure them.

Sulfanilamide was a wonder drug for treating bacterial infections. It had shown dramatic effectiveness against diseases such as meningitis and pneumonia. It saved many lives on the battlefields of World War II. Its discoverer, the German pathologist and bacteriologist Gerhard Domagk, won the Nobel Prize for Medicine in 1939, 2 years after Bobbie's death.

The tragedy was not caused by an intention to poison. It began with an intention to provide a needed cure. Sulfanilamide had been available and used effectively in tablet and powder form. In 1937, S.E. Massengill Co., a pharmaceutical company in Bristol, TN, decided to provide the drug in liquid form because one of its salesmen reported a demand for it in southern states. Harold Cole Watkins, Massengill's chief chemist and pharmacist, found that sulfanilamide would dissolve in diethylene glycol and he created elixir sulfanilamide. The mixture was tested for flavor, appearance, and fragrance but not for toxicity. As a result, the company did not notice that diethylene glycol, a colorless and odorless liquid with a sweetish taste, was actually a deadly poison until it was too late (Ballentine, 1981).

"A few simple tests on experimental animals would have demonstrated the lethal properties of the elixir," wrote Carol Ballentine, a staff writer in the Office of Public Affairs of the Food and Drug Administration (FDA) in 1981. "Even a review of the current existing scientific literature would have shown that other studies—such as those reported in several medical journals—had indicated that diethylene glycol was toxic and could cause kidney damage or failure." But back then the law did not require pharmaceutical companies to study the adverse effects of drugs, nor did it "prohibit the sale of dangerous, untested, or poisonous drugs" (Ballentine, 1981).

The company denied any legal responsibility for the mass poisoning. Dr. Samuel Evans Massengill, owner of the company, was quoted as saying: "We have been supplying a legitimate professional demand and not once could have foreseen the unlooked-for results. I do not feel that there was any responsibility on our part" (Ballentine, 1981). The chemist, Harold Watkins, who created the drug committed suicide after learning about the tragedy.

The tragedy, the elixir sulfanilamide disaster, pushed Congress to pass the Food, Drug, and Cosmetic Act of 1938, ending a 5-year bitter legislative battle. President Franklin Roosevelt signed the bill on June 25, 1938. The law, for the first time, required drug manufacturers "to provide scientific proof that new products could be safely used before putting them on the market," wrote FDA historian Wallace F. Janssen (1981). The safety requirement protected America 25 years later from the thalidomide disaster that resulted in over 10,000 babies born with deformed limbs in Europe and other regions.

### The Thalidomide Tragedy

Thalidomide was an anticonvulsive drug developed in the 1950s in West Germany. The drug was not effective in treating convulsions in epileptics. Instead, researchers found that it was very effective in inducing sleep and resulting in relaxation. The soothing, calming, and sleep-inducing effects of thalidomide made it a popular tranquilizer and sleeping pill in the postwar era when sleeplessness was widespread. Thalidomide also became popular with pregnant women because it alleviated morning sickness.

Thalidomide resulted in "history's greatest medical tragedy," according to Trent Stephens and Rock Brynner, authors of *Dark Remedy: The Impact of Thalidomide and Its Revival as a Vital Medicine* (2009, p. 9). Shortly after thalidomide went on the market, reports of side effects began to emerge. Side effects included dizziness, balance disturbances, lowered blood pressure, memory loss, constipation, trembling, hangover, and allergic reactions. But the company ignored these early reports as they did in the clinical trials. While these side effects were reported and ignored, thalidomide was causing a much bigger tragedy: babies born with malformed limbs—shortened, absent, or flipper-like limbs. In total, over 10,000 babies were born with disabilities caused by thalidomide worldwide, except in the United States, where only a few infants were affected due to the distribution of thalidomide directly to patients.

The United States was not affected thanks to the 1938 law and the wisdom and courage of Dr. Frances O. Kelsey, a Canadian working for the FDA. Kelsey relied on the law to refuse approving thalidomide for the U.S. market despite great pressures from drug companies. For her key role in protecting Americans from the dangers of the drug, Kelsey was awarded the Distinguished Federal Civilian Service Award by President John F. Kennedy in 1962. In the same year, the law was amended when Congress unanimous-ly passed the Drug Amendments of 1962. The most significant change in the new law is the requirement for efficacy. Prior to marketing, drug manufac-turers must provide scientific evidence that the product is effective, because "no drug is truly safe unless it is also effective" (Janssen, 1981).

## Modern Medicine

The acute concern about effects and side effects (safety and efficacy) is now codified in laws and regulations. In the development and research of medi-cal interventions, whether new drugs or medical procedures, it has become standard practice to weigh the risks against the product's effectiveness. The FDA requires, prior to research on a new drug or "investigating new drug (IND)," that sponsors must "notify FDA and all participating investigators, in a written IND safety report, of any adverse experience associated with the use of the drug that was both serious and unexpected, and any find-ing from tests in laboratory animals that suggested a significant risk for human subjects" (U.S. Department of Health and Human Services, Food and Drug Administration, Center for Drug Evaluation and Research, Center for Biologics Evaluation and Research, 2012, p. 2). Clinical trials, the next phase of development, have similar requirements. Even after a drug is ap-proved, research on side effects continues, and the FDA continues to watch and actively encourage the reporting of previously unidentified side effects.

*After a drug is approved, research on side effects continues.*

Today, it is universally accepted in medicine that any intervention can have unwanted effects that can damage the person it intends to heal. Medical research thus considers benefits and risks to be fundamentally inseparable: They are two sides of the same coin. When studying and reporting benefits or effectiveness, one also must study and report risks. This mindset and as-sociated practices form the foundation of modern medicine and have been shown to have tremendous value to the progress of medicine.

First, studying and reporting side effects in medicine minimizes potential damages and even saves lives by preventing products that may be effective but pose high health risks from entering the market. For example, the global pharmaceutical giant Pfizer terminated the development of torcetrapib, a drug that early studies showed to be effective in preventing heart attacks and strokes, because it triggered a higher rate of chest pains and heart fail-ure than was found in the control group during clinical trials (Ginsberg & Kingston, 2014). Although the termination meant that Pfizer lost its more than $800 million investment, it likely saved many lives.

Moreover, considering side effects also helps advance the field. Medical research is not always about finding more effective treatment; it is also about minimizing side effects. Discovering new treatments that may be equally or less effective than existing ones but cause less severe or fewer side effects also has motivated medical improvements. For example, aminopterin was used to treat children with leukemia but it had toxic effects, including "a troublesome stomatitis affecting the rapidly dividing lining cells of the mouth, leading to painful ulceration" (Sneader, 2005, p. 251). A new drug, methotrexate, replaced aminopterin because it caused less severe side effects. Just recently, a cooling cap system was developed and approved to minimize the side effect of hair loss for breast cancer patients undergoing chemotherapy (Kaplan, 2016).

> Reading First was . . . delivered rapidly to over 1.5 million children. . . . But there was no toxicity test, no concern about side effects, and no information provided . . . about its potential risks.

The studying and reporting of both effects and side effects help consumers make informed decisions. Doctors and patients can use the information to weigh the benefits and risks. Some treatments may be more effective, but their side effects are more severe. While a treatment may be less effective, its adverse effects also may be less severe. Thus, in some cases making choices about a medical treatment is extremely difficult. But being fully informed of known risks associated with the treatment definitely helps in these difficult times. This is why all medical products are required to disclose their side effects and information about their effectiveness. This is true even for common over the counter drugs such as cold medicine. When you buy a bottle of Ibuprofen, for example, the label clearly indicates its effectiveness in relieving pain and reducing fever, but also its potential to cause severe allergic reactions and stomach bleeding.

## MOVING BEYOND RCT: A SUMMARY

Reading First was the first major national reading intervention delivered rapidly to over 1.5 million children in the nation's most disadvantaged schools. It was the first program that supposedly was based on scientific evidence. But there was no toxicity test, no concern about side effects, and no information provided to parents, students, teachers, and the public about its potential risks. In many ways, it was like the elixir sulfanilamide prepared by Harold Cole Watkins of S.E. Massengill in 1937. Sulfanilamide was effective and safe, but the addition was poisonous. It was also like thalidomide, safe and effective for some people, but dangerous to others, especially pregnant women. The individual studies examined by the National Reading Panel may have shown positive effects on some outcomes, but Reading First could have caused damage to others, such as loss of motivation and interest. It may have worked for some students, and could have hurt others. It may have been a complete waste of time for some students, who could

*Education can hurt and help at the same time, just like medicine.*

have benefited from other inventions, a potential damage akin to misdiagnosis of a disease or misapplication of medicine. But the potential damages were never examined by the reviewed studies and the Panel could not have known about or considered them.

This is because education does not have a tradition of considering side effects, let alone studying and reporting them. To move education into a field using scientific evidence, we need educational research to not only use scientific methods such as RCT, but also adopt the mindset that education can hurt and help at the same time, just like medicine.

# CHAPTER 3

# Unproductive Successes and Productive Failures
## Direct Instruction and Classroom Side Effects

"Early reading was associated with early educational success, but was also associated with worse long-term outcomes including less overall educational attainment, worse teenage and adult adjustment, and increased alcohol use," concluded Margaret Kern and Howard S. Friedman (2009, p. 427). The two psychologists from the University of California, Riverside, reached this conclusion based on a study that followed the entire life span of more than 1,000 of the "smartest" individuals in the world. They reported their findings in an article published in the *Journal of Applied Developmental Psychology* in 2009.

> "Early reading was associated with early educational success, but was also associated with worse long-term outcomes."

The study started in the 1920s with Stanford professor Lewis Terman, the developer of the widely used Stanford–Binet IQ test. Terman recruited over 1,500 "most intelligent" children to join the Terman Life Cycle Study of Children with High Ability. The children were born around 1910 and had to have an IQ score of 135 or above to be included in the project. They were followed throughout their lives, with data collected about their conditions every 5 or 10 years until their deaths.

Friedman and colleagues examined the data from the Terman project. While the data showed correlation, not direct causation, they came to the conclusion that early literacy was negatively associated with important indicators of life quality, such as social–emotional well-being and adjustment in the long term. They also discovered that early school entry had similar negative associations with life quality later on.

Does this mean early reading causes damage in the long term? We cannot be sure because the study was not a randomized controlled experiment on the effect of early reading on life quality. Other factors undoubtedly would come into play. However, it does cast doubt about the widespread belief that early reading ability set people on an upward trajectory for life (The Annie E. Casey Foundation, 2010, 2013). It at least suggests the existence of the possibility that efforts to boost early reading could backfire in the long term.

Unfortunately, studies like this are rare in education. The majority of studies in education are concerned with the immediate effectiveness of interventions. They typically are conducted to prove or disprove the effectiveness of a certain intervention in achieving short-term instructional outcomes, with little concern about whether the immediate success may be accompanied by failure in the long run. The effectiveness often is measured by the degree to which students can demonstrate their mastery of prescribed knowledge and skills. So long as the results show improvement, the intervention is deemed effective, although the effects may come at the cost of other, perhaps more important outcomes. Such is the case with direct instruction.

Direct instruction, also called explicit teaching or intentional teaching, is a teaching approach that "is skills-oriented, and the teaching practices it implies are teacher-directed" (Carnine, Silbert, Kame'enui, & Tarver, 2004, p. 11; see also Carnine, 2000). It is characterized by the explicit teaching of skills and content through instruction by teachers. The content and skills typically are broken down into small units and sequenced deliberately (Carnine et al., 2004; Rosenshine, 1978, 2008, 2009). There are two forms of direct instruction. One is the generic lowercase direct instruction, which includes a set of instructional practices that follow the general principles described above (Rosenshine, 1978, 2008, 2009). The other is the uppercase Direct Instruction (DI), a specific teaching program following and going beyond the generic principles of direct instruction, providing teachers with scripts for instruction from which they are not to deviate.

> *Project Follow Through ultimately became an experiment to test the effectiveness of different models in improving educational outcomes for disadvantaged youth.*

Direct instruction, in both lower- and uppercase forms, has been the major contender in recent years, against the child-centered models, for dominance in classrooms. It has been battled over in both the reading and math wars. To move forward, we should not continue the unproductive quarrel over whether direct instruction is effective, but rather should consider in which areas it is effective *and* whether it has long-term adverse side effects. The rest of the chapter uses the history of Direct Instruction to illustrate how understanding the effects and side effects of direct instruction can advance education.

## THE GRIEVANCE OF DIRECT INSTRUCTION

Direct Instruction made its debut in 1968 as Direct Instruction System for Teaching Arithmetic and Reading, or DISTAR, as one of the 22 instructional models included in Project Follow Through (Bereiter & Kurland, 1981; Stebbins, 1977), ostensibly the largest education experiment sponsored by the U.S. federal government. Initially proposed as a social service program to "follow through" on the popular Head Start program introduced in 1965 as a part of President Lyndon Johnson's war on poverty, Project Follow Through ultimately became an experiment to test the effectiveness of different models in improving educational outcomes for disadvantaged youth. The experiment started in 1968 and concluded in 1976, although the program continued into the 1990s. The experiment cost nearly $1 billion and involved hundreds of thousands of children in over 100 communities. A $30 million national evaluation was conducted and four volumes of reports were published.

### Undisputed Winner

DISTAR emerged to be the "undisputed winner" in the experiment, according to its co-inventor Siegfried Engelmann, who recounted DI's successful showing in Project Follow Through in 2007: "Not only were we first in adjusted scores and first in percentile scores for basic skills, cognitive skills, and perceptions children had of themselves, we were first in spelling, first with sites that had a Head Start preschool, first in sites that started in K, and first in sites that started in grade 1" (p. 228).

> DISTAR emerged to be the "undisputed winner" in the experiment, according to its co-inventor.

The list of evidence of success goes on: "Our third-graders who went through only three years (grades 1–3) were, on average, over a year ahead of children in other models who went through four years—grades K–3" (Engelmann, 2007, pp. 228–229). Furthermore, Engelmann wrote: "We were first with Native Americans, first with non-English speakers, first in rural areas, first in urban areas, first with Whites, first with Blacks, first with the lowest disadvantaged children, and first with high performers" (p. 229).

Engelmann and associates were absolutely convinced that they had developed the most effective teaching approach. "For the first time in the history of compensatory education, DI showed that long-range, stable, replicable, and highly positive results were possible with at-risk children of different types and in different settings," wrote Engelmann (2007, p. 229), asserting that all instructional programs before DI were "a phantom" and their effectiveness "a function of fortuitous happenings, a measurement artifact, or a hoax" (p. 229). Moreover, they believed that DI was effective for all students, in all subjects, for developing both basic skills and high-level cognitive skills. It was also effective in the affective domains because it made children confident (Engelmann, 2007; National Institute for Direct Instruction, 2014). Best of all, Engelmann believed that DI did not turn children into robots.

## Underwhelming Reception

Confident of their approach, the developers of DISTAR were eager to have the model be widely disseminated. As soon as the results were made public in 1977, co-developer Wesley C. Becker, a psychology professor, published an article about DI and its stunning performance in Project Follow Through in *Harvard Educational Review*, hoping to attract attention. "Wes antici-pated that the article would stimulate great interest," recounts Engelmann in his 2007 book. But it did not happen. "Instead, there was almost no re-sponse—no revelations reported by readers who realized that the practices they espoused had led to unnecessary failure or revelations that DI present-ed a better way to solve problems that had been haunting school districts since the Coleman Report"[1] (p. 231).

The developers of DISTAR also had expected Project Follow Through to declare their approach the only effective one and to provide funding for national dissemination. That did not happen, either. Instead DI was treated the same as all the other instructional models. Moreover, Project Follow Through changed from em-phasizing sponsors of instructional models to individual schools. Schools applied for funds to disseminate their "successful" programs. Apparently, the programs that were validated as successful included DI and other models. In the end, out of the more than 200 schools validated to disseminate their programs through the National Diffusion Network, only three were DI schools (Engelmann, 2007).

> People involved in education do respect evidence but may have different views about what constitutes good evidence and how . . . evidence should be interpreted.

The developers of DI were naturally unhappy. They protested. They wrote letters to the director of Project Follow Through. They contacted politicians, including then–Oregon Senator Bob Packwood, who intervened and received a response from the U.S. Commissioner of Education. But still,

---

1. The Coleman Report (Coleman et al., 1966) is one of the most influential and controversial studies concerning education in the United States. The study found enor-mous racial gaps in educational achievement.

DI was not treated as the "undisputed winner" and promoted as the only effective approach nationally, as Engelmann and associates would have liked (Engelmann, 2007).

For the next few decades, DI proponents continued to promote the approach as the most effective (Becker & Gersten, 1982; Engelmann, 2007; Gersten & Keating, 1987; T. Kim & Axelrod, 2005). They conducted numerous empirical studies and gathered mountains of evidence in support of DI's effectiveness. They published books and journal articles, and even set up their own press and journals to disseminate the evidence and advocate for DI's adoption. They organized hundreds of conferences and training programs for educators to spread DI. These efforts certainly helped expand the acceptance of DI, but they failed to put DI in every classroom in America, not even with the help of No Child Left Behind and Reading First, which explicitly favored approaches like DI.

### Sore and Unenlightened Losers

Why has "the most effective" approach for educating children not been widely disseminated? DI advocates have put forth various theories. They believe there was a conspiracy against DI. Engelmann (2007) charged the federal Office of Education, which administered Project Follow Through, with "conspiracy to propagate lies and intellectual casuistry" by not recognizing DI as the most effective model discovered through Project Follow Through and consequently not promoting it as such in subsequent funding decisions (p. 252). Engelmann also named the Ford Foundation as a co-conspirator against DI for commissioning an independent review of the national evaluation of Project Follow Through, because the review was critical of the original evaluation and conclusion (House, Glass, McLean, & Walker, 1978).

As to why there was a conspiracy against DI, "sore loser" reaction was the answer from DI advocates. They believed that Project Follow Through showed that models that focused on explicit instruction of basic skills were clearly superior to "child-centered" models. However, the education establishment, which was deeply entrenched in the "child-centered" philosophy, was unwilling to face the results, mounted an attack against DI, and prevented the wide dissemination of the findings of Project Follow Through (Bereiter & Kurland, 1981; Carnine, 2000; Engelmann, 2007; T. Kim & Axelrod, 2005; Watkins, 1995, 1997). For example, Kathy L. Watkins (1995), a recipient of the Association for Direct Instruction's Excellence in Education Award and an inductee of the Association for Direct Instruction Hall of Fame, wrote:

Thus, the data from Follow Through fail to support the philosophy that dominates colleges of education. This obviously made it difficult for educators to accept the Follow Through findings and they responded by discrediting the evaluation as well as by voicing specific objections about the Direct Instruction model or questioning the values of the model.

Advocates viewed all and any criticism of DI as the result of an unenlightened field that disregarded scientific research in favor of ideological faith. Douglas Carnine, an adamant advocate of DI, wrote a paper entitled *Why Education Experts Resist Effective Practices (and What It Would Take to Make Education More Like Medicine)* in 2000 for the conservative think tank Thomas B. Fordham Institute. He asserted that the education establishment was so indoctrinated in the "romantic notion" that children can learn naturally that it "has closed the minds of many experts to actual research findings about effective approaches to educating children"(p. 8). Accordingly, Carnine (2000) criticizes education as "an immature profession, one that lacks a solid scientific base and has less respect for evidence than for opinion and ideology" (p. 8).

## EFFECTIVENESS VERSUS EFFECTS OF DIRECT INSTRUCTION

Carnine is correct, to a degree. Education as a field indeed lacks a solid scientific base but it does not necessarily have "less respect for evidence than for opinion and ideology." People involved in education do respect evidence but may have different views about what constitutes good evidence and how certain evidence should be interpreted. Moreover, educators are not aware of the difference between effectiveness and effects. Effectiveness is a measure of the extent to which an outcome is successfully produced, while effect is the outcome. While DI proponents have argued for DI's effectiveness, its opponents have been concerned about its effects because they don't necessarily agree that the outcomes (effects) DI is effective in producing are as important as other outcomes. In some cases, the more effective DI is, the more concerned we should become because it may be effective in causing unwanted effects. Skeptics of DI thus have been concerned about its undetected and unreported adverse effects on children (Schweinhart & Weikart, 1997; Schweinhart, Weikart, & Larner, 1986).

*It is precisely the care for evidence that led to the reanalysis and reinterpretation of the data from Project Follow Through.*

## Defending DI's Effectiveness: The "He Said, She Said" of Project Follow Through

It is unfair to accuse DI critics or the education establishment of having no respect for evidence. Quite the contrary, they all care about evidence. It is precisely the care for evidence that led to the reanalysis and reinterpretation of the data from Project Follow Through, which DI proponents have been using as their major supportive evidence.

The official evaluation of Project Follow Through was conducted by Abt Associates, which released their final report in 1977. The main findings include:

- The effectiveness of each Follow Through model varied substantially from site group to site group; overall model averages varied little in comparison.
- Models that emphasize basic skills succeeded better than other models in helping children gain these skills.
- Where models have put their primary emphasis elsewhere than on the basic skills, the children they served have tended to score lower on tests of these skills than they would have done without Follow Through.
- No type of model was notably more successful than the others in raising scores on cognitive conceptual skills.
- Models that emphasized basic skills produced better results on tests of self-concept than did other models. (Stebbins, 1977, pp. 135–147)

Engelmann (2007) did not like the conclusions because they did not directly declare DI the clear winner. They did not explicitly state that DI was the most effective model in achievement scores in all three areas: basic skills, cognitive conceptual skills, and self-concept. He complained that the analysis "was bent to be unkind to DI" (p. 225). Nonetheless, he believed that the numbers did not lie, and according to his analysis and interpretation, DI sites indeed showed more improvement in all three areas than schools using other models.

More "unkind" analyses came soon after the release of the evaluation report. The review commissioned by the Ford Foundation and conducted by a panel of leading education experts, composed of professors Ernest House at the University of Illinois, Gene Glass at the University of Colorado–Boulder, Leslie D. McLean at the Ontario Institute for Studies in Education, and Decker F. Walker at Stanford University, pointed out that even the original "unkind" conclusion that basic skills models were more effective was erroneous (House et al., 1978). The reviewers believed one finding in the original report was valid: The effectiveness of a model varied a great deal from one site to another. Thus, they concluded that the differences in individual teachers, students, neighborhoods, and communities in different locations mattered a lot more to student achievement than instructional models did (House et al., 1978).

*The review commissioned by the Ford Foundation ... pointed out that even the original "unkind" conclusion that basic skills models were more effective was erroneous.*

House and colleagues also raised questions about measurements, arguing that some very important outcomes, such as improvements in personality and character, the ability to read aloud, and the ability to write a story, were not measured. In addition, some of the instruments used were not sensitive to instruction and were unsophisticated. They also criticized the analyses as arbitrary and unwise. Finally, they argued that the scope of the measurement was biased because the evaluation did not assess all model goals (House et al., 1978).

Mary Kennedy at the U.S. Office of Education (1978) performed another analysis of the results of Project Follow Through that showed that the effectiveness of DI was not as great as its advocates claimed. She found that "the two models with at least one sizeable positive effect were both structured classroom approaches [DI and behavioral analysis], while the three with a sizeable negative effect were relatively unstructured approaches" (p. 5). However, she noted that "sizeable effects do not appear on all outcomes," contrary to what Engelmann concluded.

Carl Bereiter, professor of education at Ontario Institute for Studies in Education, rushed to the defense of DI. Bereiter, who had worked with Engelmann in the early development of DI at the University of Illinois at Urbana–Champaign (UIUC), and Midian Kurland at UIUC reanalyzed the data (Bereiter & Kurland, 1981). They first disputed the finding of the original report and the House panel that the within-model variations across sites were larger than the variations between models. They found significant differences between models. DI and behavior analysis, another basic skills model, were the winners in producing improvements in all achievement subtests (Bereiter & Kurland, 1981).

Kathy Watkins, a DI proponent, revisited the Project Follow Through data and history in her publications in 1995 and 1997. In both publications, she presented DI as the most effective instructional model. She contended that the lack of wider dissemination of DI was the result of resistance on the part of the establishment, which ignored or trivialized the findings of Project Follow Through (Watkins, 1995, 1997).

Education historian Maris Vinovskis at the University of Michigan reviewed the various analyses and reanalyses of Project Follow Through in his book *History and Educational Policymaking* (1999). He noted the controversies around the different interpretations of effects or lack thereof, sources of effects, and the general impact of the project. He found no indication that there was consensus that DI was indeed the most effective approach on all outcomes measured in Project Follow Through. But at the same time, there was no evidence to discredit the effectiveness of DI in some domains, especially basic skills in reading and math.

Evidence of the effectiveness of direct instruction, in both its uppercase and lowercase forms, continued to be produced after Project Follow Through. Today there are indeed mountains of evidence that support direct instruction as an effective instructional approach (Adams & Engelmann, 1996; Becker & Gersten, 1982; Brent & DiObilda, 1993; Dean & Kuhn, 2007; Gunn, Biglan, Smolkowski, & Ary, 2000; L. A. Meyer, 1984; Peterson, 1979; Roehler & Duffy, 1982; Schwerdt & Wuppermann, 2011; Slavin, 2008; Stockard, 2010; Swanson & Sachse-Lee, 2000). The National Institute for Direct Instruction published a 102-page bibliography of writings on the effectiveness of Direct Instruction in 2015, each page containing about 12 entries.

## Genuine Concerns About Side Effects or Manufactured Myths

But criticism of DI, and the unwillingness of many educators to accept it as an effective educational approach, comes from much more than uncertainty about its effectiveness. It originates from a broader suspicion of DI's claim that it benefits all students, is effective for all outcomes, and works in all settings. DI proponents have categorically viewed the criticism as biased, unenlightened, and ideologically driven myths. They have put in much effort to debunk the myths (Adams & Engelmann, 1996; Tarver, 1998).

The myths DI proponents have set out to debunk exemplify the concerns about DI's effects and effectiveness. These "myths" are roughly related to concerns in two areas: outcomes and students. DI critics are most concerned about DI's outcomes. DI advocates have claimed that it is effective in effecting positive changes in all outcome domains (National Institute for Direct Instruction, 2014), but is that true? Could it actually cause damage?

> *Criticism of DI . . . comes from much more than uncertainty about its effectiveness.*

For example, six out of the 10 myths University of Wisconsin professor Sara Tarver tried to debunk in her 1998 article "Myths and Truths About Direct Instruction" are related to outcomes:

Myth #1: DI may be effective at teaching very rudimentary academic skills but it is not effective at teaching problem solving or promoting higher order cognitive learning.

Myth #2: DI reading programs may be effective at teaching decoding and word recognition, but they are not effective at teaching reading comprehension.

Myth #4: DI has a detrimental effect on students' self concept or self esteem and on attitudes toward learning.

Myth #8: The rigid structure of DI lessons fosters dependence on the teacher; students taught with DI are not capable of functioning successfully in independent situations.

Myth #9: Although DI produces academic gains in the early grades, it has no lasting effects on students' success in school.

Myth #10: DI's structure and scripted lessons stifle teachers' and students' creativity. (pp. 18–22)

The second area DI skeptics are concerned about is whether DI works for all students, as its proponents claim (National Institute for Direct Instruction, 2014). Three out of the 10 myths Tarver (1998) attempts to dispel are about DI's effectiveness for different populations of students:

Myth #5: DI may be appropriate for disadvantaged students, but it is not appropriate for other students who are at risk of failure in school and it is not appropriate for average and above-average achievers.

Myth #6: DI is not appropriate for students with dyslexia because it is not multisensory.

Myth #7: DI may be appropriate for students in the early grades, but it is not appropriate for middle school students, high school students, and adults. (pp. 18–22)

Gary Adams and Siegfried Engelmann also wrote about the myths about DI in their book *Research on Direct Instruction: 25 Years Beyond DISTAR* in 1996. Four out of their eight myths are about outcomes:

Myth 3: DI eschews developmental progression and developmental theory.

Myth 4: DI's scripted presentations and predetermined lessons stifle the teacher's creativity.

Myth 6: DI promotes passive learning.

Myth 7: DI ignores individual differences. One is about appropriateness for different populations of students and the rest [are] about the characteristics and procedures of the program (Adams & Engelmann, 1996, pp. 25–32).

In their efforts to debunk the myths, DI proponents relied more on *a priori* reasoning and general statements than on empirical evidence. For example, in an attempt to debunk the so-called myth about DI's ineffectiveness in teaching comprehension, Tarver (1998) presents "Truth #2. DI reading programs have been used successfully to teach comprehension as well as decoding and recognition" (p. 19). She then explains how the DI reading program Reading Mastery VI teaches reasoning skills, but she cites no empirical evidence that it is actually effective. She admits that it "is accurate to say the evidence of the effectiveness of DI comprehension instruction is not as extensive as that for DI decoding instruction" (p. 19). In conclusion, she argues that "the evidence supporting DI comprehension instruction is substantial," without citing any source. Interestingly, there is sufficient empirical evidence suggesting that strategies that improve decoding skills do not necessarily lead to improvement in reading comprehension (Cummins, 2007).

DI advocates also tried to conduct empirical studies to show the model's long-term benefits, which also have been questioned by critics. In 1982, Wesley Becker and Russell Gersten, proponents of DI, published the results of a study of the later effects of DISTAR in the *American Educational Research Journal*. Essentially, the study found that students who had received the DI program from 1st to 3rd grades retained their advantage in 5th and 6th grades over those who had not. Becker and Gersten (1982) reported consistently strong significant effects on decoding skills, consistent but less significant effects on math problem solving and spelling, and "moderate effects in most other academic domains" (p. 75). Another study conducted by Linda Meyer (1984) at UIUC produced similar findings, confirming that DI had long-term positive effects on academic outcomes.

In 1987, Russell Gersten and Thomas Keating published another follow-up study undertaken to determine whether the positive effects of DI lasted into high school. Not surprisingly, they found that DI produced long-term benefits: Students who were in the DISTAR program from 1st to 3rd grades did better than those who did not experience the program. They "scored higher on standardized tests, dropped out less, and applied to college more often than did students in comparison groups" (Gersten & Keating, 1987, p. 28). The authors claim that "in each of the four communities we studied, we found positive long-term effects for students in the direct instruction programs. These effects were consistent at all places and among all groups." However, they contradict their claim in the next sentence: "In some places, such as Finley, the effects were in achievement but not in dropout rate; while in others, such as Williamsburg County, they were in graduation rates but not achievement" (p. 31).

These follow-up studies essentially confirmed earlier findings about DI. It was effective in some domains: basic skills in reading and math. But its proponents overstated its effects in the affective domain. As a result, neither the articles aiming to debunk the myths nor the follow-up studies worked to persuade more people to accept DI as an effective teaching model for all outcomes and students, and as a model without any negative side effects.

### Emerging Evidence of Side Effects

Evidence of side effects gradually emerged. Because there was no tradition of studying side effects, few studies paid attention to the potential side effects of DI or other interventions. Most of the concerns about DI's potential side effects were theoretical speculations. The first empirical study to show possible negative side effects of DI appeared in the journal *Early Childhood Research Quarterly* (Schweinhart et al., 1986).

The study started in 1967 in Ypsilanti, MI. Psychologist David P. Weikart and his colleagues decided to assess the relative effects of three different instructional models on preschoolers: High/Scope, a child-centered discovery learning approach developed by Weikart; Direct Instruction; and traditional nursery school. Sixty-eight 3- to 4-year-old children living in poverty were assigned to each condition using a stratified random-assignment procedure. The children experienced the programs for 1 or 2 years. They were followed through later ages.

The study found that through age 10, the only noticeable difference among the three groups was that at age 5, children in the DI condition had a significantly higher mean IQ score than those in the traditional nursery condition. But through age 15, a shocking difference was observed when the researchers expanded the measurement of outcomes to include community behavior. They found that the DI group reported committing more acts of misconduct, two and a half times more, than the High/Scope group. Additionally, the DI group reported that they were not as well thought of by their families as were those in the other two groups. The DI group also had fewer members reporting engagement in positive social activities (Schweinhart & Weikart, 1997).

This study drew swift criticism from proponents of Direct Instruction. Carl Bereiter quickly and rightly pointed out the possible conflict of interests of the researchers, who were the developers and owners of High/Scope, which was and still is a major competitor of DI. High/Scope also was not shown to be effective in the outcomes measured in Project Follow Through. Moreover, Bereiter (1986) challenged the validity of the findings, pointing out flaws in data collection and analysis.

About 10 years later, in 1997, the researchers published their latest findings. The children were then 22 years old. This follow-up study was more valid methodologically and addressed the challenges raised by Bereiter. Among other results, the study (Schweinhart & Weikart, 1997) found:

- The High/Scope group did better than the Direct Instruction group in life quality outcomes such as highest year of schooling planned, higher percentage living with spouse, fewer sources of irritation, less self-reported misconduct at age 15, fewer felony arrests, and fewer arrests for property crimes.
- The nursery school group had fewer suspensions from work and fewer felony arrests at age 22 than the Direct Instruction group.
- Both the High/Scope and nursery school groups experienced fewer years of identified emotional impairment or disturbance and involved in more volunteer work than the Direct Instruction group.

There are a number of issues that threaten the validity of the High/Scope studies. First, the conflict of interests was obvious. The researchers all had a vested interest, both ideologically and financially, in the success of High/Scope and failure of Direct Instruction because they are direct competitors. David Weikart was the initiator of High/Scope and Lawrence Schweinhart was the president of High/Scope Educational Research Foundation at the time. Second, the sample size was extremely small. With a total of 68 children placed in three conditions, each group had only about 23 members. With natural attrition over the years, only 52 participants were included in the 1997 study. Although the researchers recognized the limitation of a small sample and took that into consideration in their analysis, it nonetheless significantly limits the study's generalizability.

## EFFECTS AND SIDE EFFECTS OF DIRECT INSTRUCTION

There is more evidence of side effects of direct instruction. Despite DI advocates' claim that DI does not stifle creativity, a review article by Penelope L. Peterson in 1979 found the contrary. DI indeed could suppress creativity and problem solving while boosting achievement test scores. After reviewing over 200 studies, she concluded:

With direct or traditional teaching, students tend to do slightly better on achievement tests, but they do slightly worse on tests of abstract thinking, such as creativity and problem solving. Conversely, with open teaching, students do somewhat worse on achievement tests, but they do somewhat better on creativity and problem solving. Furthermore, open approaches excel direct or traditional approaches in increasing students' attitudes toward school and toward the teacher and in improving students' independence and curiosity. In all these cases, the effects were small. (p. 47)

## Suppressing Curiosity and Creativity

Peterson's observations are theoretically plausible. Direct instruction can be effective "in promoting rapid and efficient learning of target material" (Bonawitza et al., 2011, p. 322), but it can negatively impact creativity because "instruction necessarily limits the range of hypotheses children consider" (p. 322) and their attempt to explore novel situations. This reasoning was supported by evidence from two experimental studies. Findings of both studies were published in the journal *Cognition* (Bonawitza et al., 2011; Buchsbauma, Gopnika, Griffiths, & Shaftob, 2011).

In one study, Elizabeth Bonawitza at the University of California, Berkeley, and colleagues conducted two experiments among preschoolers. In the first experiment, 85 preschoolers aged from 48 to 72 months were randomly assigned into four conditions: one pedagogical and three non-pedagogical, which included interrupted, naïve, and baseline. The task was to play with a novel toy. In the *pedagogical* condition, the experimenter acted like a teacher using direct instruction. She told the children, "Look at my toy! This is my toy. I'm going to show you how my toy works. Watch this!" She then proceeded to demonstrate one of the multiple ways of playing with the toy. The *interrupted* condition had exactly the same treatment except that the experimenter interrupted herself and moved away from the scene immediately after the demonstration. In the *naïve* condition, the experimenter told the children she had just found the toy and as if by accident discovered the way to play with the toy by saying, "Huh! Did you see that? Let me try to do that!" She then performed the same action, but as if it was an accidental discovery of the function. In the *baseline* condition, the experimenter did not initially demonstrate the use of the toy. She simply called children's attention to the toy by saying, "Wow, see this toy? Look at this!" To match the amount of familiarization time in other conditions, she looked at the toy for about 2 seconds and put it back on the table. In all conditions, after the initial introduction, the experimenter encouraged the children to figure out how the toy worked and then left them to play with it (Bonawitza et al., 2011, p. 322).

The researchers video-recorded all sessions and compared children's to-tal time playing, the number of unique actions performed, the proportion of time spent on the demonstrated function, and the total number of functions discovered. Their data suggest

> that teaching constrains children's exploration and discovery. Children who were taught a function of a toy performed fewer kinds of actions of the toy and discovered fewer of its other functions, than children who did not receive a pedagogical demonstration, even though all children were explicitly encouraged to explore the toy. (Bonawitza et al., 2011, p. 325)

The results of the second experiment confirmed findings of the first. It also found that children could infer pedagogical intentions. In other words, even if children are not directly instructed but are given the opportunity to overhear instructions to their peers, they believe teaching is happening and that they should follow the instructor.

The other study (Buchsbauma et al., 2011) provides more evidence that direct instruction is efficient and effective in teaching targeted knowl-edge, but inhibits curiosity and creativity. The study also was conducted with a group of preschoolers using toys. The results show that in situations where the experimenter adopted the role of an instructor and di-rectly gave instructions and demonstrations, children were more likely to imitate the in-structor than in other conditions. But they were found to be less likely to explore and come up with novel solutions (Buchsbauma et al., 2011).

*Drect instruction is efficient and effective in teaching targeted knowledge, but inhibits curiosity and creativity.*

Similar findings are reported in math learning (Kapur, 2014). Manu Kapur, currently professor and chair of learning sciences and higher edu-cation at ETH Zurich, Switzerland, conducted an experiment that found students generated more solutions to problems before instruction than after. Students who received instruction first tended to produce only the correct solutions they were taught. Kapur (2016) thus suggests that instruction seems to constrain students' search for novel solutions, which is necessary for creativity and inventiveness.

### Unproductive Successes

Kapur (2016) used "unproductive success" to characterize direct instruction in a recent article in *Educational Psychologist*. According to Kapur, un-productive success is intervention that "may maximize performance in the shorter term without maximizing learning in the longer term . . . it is possible for students to show high performance on memory tasks or carrying out problem-solving procedures without a commensurable understanding of what it is that they are doing" (p. 290).

Kapur substantiated his assertion with empirical evidence. He conducted a quasi-experimental study where students were placed in two different conditions: direct instruction, in which students received teacher-led lectures guided by the course workbook, and productive failure, in which first students were asked to solve complex math problems and then the teacher provided explanations of "canonical" solutions. Kapur found that students in the direct instruction condition were initially more successful in solving well-structured problems (Kapur & Bielaczyc, 2012). However, in the end, their performance on tasks that required deeper conceptual understanding was inferior to that of students in the productive failure condition.

Another form of unproductive success of direct instruction is that it may be more effective in teaching knowledge and skills than discovery learning, but the knowledge and skills acquired through direct instruction do not transfer to authentic contexts. In an attempt to counter this claim about direct instruction, Carnegie Mellon University psychologist David Klahr and Director of Applied Research and Evaluation at the University of Pittsburgh Milena Nigam conducted an experimental study on the effectiveness of direct instruction and discovery learning in science learning. The experiment was designed to see whether direct instruction, which previously had been confirmed through experiments to be more effective than discovery learning in teaching children an elementary school science objective—control-of-variables strategy (CVS) (Klahr & Nigam, 2004)—would result in a level of transfer to authentic contexts similar to that in discovery learning.

*Another form of unproductive success of direct instruction is that . . . knowledge and skills acquired through direct instruction do not transfer to authentic contexts.*

The results show that direct instruction was much more effective in teaching the 3rd- and 4th-graders the concept of CVS, and the children who learned the concept through direct instruction were equally as good at applying the concept to authentic contexts the next day as children who learned the concept through discovery learning. Thus, Klahr and Nigam concluded that how children learned a concept (learning path) does not affect their ability to apply the concept. Hence, direct instruction is superior

*The initial success of DI comes at the cost of inferior performance on transfer later.*

to discovery learning because it can produce more successful learning without affecting the longer-term goal of transfer (Klahr & Nigam, 2004).

This conclusion was soon proved to be wrong. David Dean Jr. and Deanna Kuhn, two psychologists at Teachers College, Columbia University, conducted an almost identical study to that by Klahr and Nigam, except that they followed the progress over an extended period of time. They found that "brief direct instruction is capable of producing a significant level of correct performance with respect to the control of variables strategy, immediately following instruction" (Dean & Kuhn, 2007, p. 394). However, at week 11, DI's effects began to disappear. The performance of the direct instruction group on transfer was significantly lower than that of the children in the comparison group at week 11 and week 17. The study shows that the immediate success of DI is unnecessary because discovery learning eventually can lead to the same level of learning. More important, the initial success of DI comes at the cost of inferior performance on transfer later (Dean & Kuhn, 2007).

## SUMMARY

Obviously, we should be very cautious about drawing any general conclusions based on just a few studies. However, the philosophy underlying the studies is what we need in educational research. An approach that simultaneously studies effects and side effects of educational interventions holds great promise to resolve long-fought battles with empirical evidence. These studies essentially confirm that DI can be effective in knowledge transmission *and* suppress creativity and curiosity at the same time. In education, we need effective ways to both transmit knowledge and foster creativity. DI has its place in education. However, its side effects need to be minimized. To advance education, it is thus important to direct efforts to exploring when DI should be used, for what purpose, and for which population, as well as strategies to mitigate its adverse effects on creativity.

More important, studies like these give consumers information to make choices. Knowing the effects and side effects of educational interventions, consumers (policymakers, educators, parents, and students) can decide what interventions and instructional methods to adopt and can understand the potential risks and benefits of their decisions. In the case of DI, if further investigations confirm that its effectiveness in promoting rapid and efficient mastery of knowledge and skills comes at the expense of creativity and curiosity, education consumers can choose whether, when, or to what extent they wish to adopt it, or whether they want to turn to discovery learning.

What is of particular importance is whether the damage to creativity and curiosity is long term and extends beyond the immediate situation. A one-time treatment of direct instruction is unlikely to inhibit children's curiosity and creativity for life. But what if children are exposed to only direct instruction for 12 years or longer? Would it cause them to become less creative?

# CHAPTER 4

# At What Cost

## Side Effects at the System Level in East Asia

"What Asian Schools Can Teach the Rest of Us" is the title of an op-ed piece by Andreas Schleicher, Director of the Organisation for Economic Co-operation and Development (OECD) Directorate of Education and Skills, published by CNN in 2016, in which he lectures Americans on why and what they should learn from East Asian education systems. In the eyes of Schleicher, the man who runs the world's largest international tests, known as the Program for International Student Assessment (PISA), East Asian education systems such as those of China, Singapore, Korea, and Japan are the best among the over 70 education systems that participated in his tests in 2015. He believes East Asian education systems hold great lessons for the rest of the world.

But the East Asians disagree. "If anything, the lesson should be the other way around. East Asia has a lot to learn from the American school system," wrote Jung-kyu Kim and Young-oak Kim, co-authors of the book *The Great Equal Society: Confucianism, China and the 21st Century* (J. Kim & Kim, 2014). "To China's educationalists the timing of the Western love affair with their system is striking," wrote Imogen West-Knights in the *Financial Times* in 2017. The Chinese are looking to the West for lessons. In fact, the entire East Asian region has been borrowing lessons from the West to improve its education (Zhao, 2015a; Zhao & Wang, 2018).

### THE SURPRISING ADMIRATION FOR EAST ASIAN EDUCATION

The East Asians are surprised by the sudden arrival of admiration from the West because the West has been, for a long time, their source of ideas for educational excellence. Except for a period before the 18th century when Europe was infatuated with the Chinese civilization (Pak, 1974), the East has been learning (or forced to learn) from the West for most of modern times, including in education. Although East Asian education today has its distinct cultural roots, the essential features, such as how education is organized and delivered and what content should be taught, are copied from the West.

But in recent years, East Asian education has become the object of idolization and source of ideas for improving education in the West and other parts of the world (Zhao, 2017). Eager admirers and learners from around the globe have come to East Asia for lessons in policy, curriculum, school management, teachers, and teaching. Academic scholars, policy wonks, journalists, and casual observers have produced numerous articles, books, documentary films, and blog posts praising East Asian education systems and making a broad range of recommendations for other systems around the world (Bieber & Martens, 2011; Darling-Hammond & Lieberman, 2012; Figazzolo, 2009; Jensen, 2012; Lamb & Fullarton, 2002; H.-D. Meyer & Benavot, 2013; National Research Council, 1999; Nelson, 2002; OECD, 2011; Schleicher, 2013; Schmidt, 1999; Tucker, 2011, 2014).

> *Admirers and learners from around the globe have come to East Asia for lessons in policy, curriculum, school management, teachers, and teaching.*

Many of the recommendations have been taken seriously and implemented. For example, the UK has decided to have half of its primary schools, about 8,000, adopt the math teaching method practiced in Hong Kong, Singapore, and Shanghai because of their performance (Telegraph Reporters, 2016). Britain also has decided to import Chinese math textbooks (Qin, 2017). Some schools in the United States have adopted Singaporean math textbooks and teaching strategies (Hu, 2010). Additionally, much of the argument for international benchmarking in the U.S. Common Core State Standards was based on the features of curriculum standards in East Asian education systems (National Governors Association Center for Best Practices & Council of Chief State School Officers, 2010). It is safe to say that East Asian education systems have had a significant impact on educational policies and practices around the world in the past 2 decades.

## EVIDENCE OF EFFECTIVENESS

The West's love affair with East Asian education is not without good reason and evidence. In fact, it is based on a large amount of evidence systematically collected over several decades. The first major pieces of evidence were presented in 1994. In the wildly influential book *The Learning Gap:*

*Why Our Schools Are Failing and What We Can Learn from Japanese and Chinese Education,* Harold Stevenson and James Stigler, educational researchers at the University of Michigan, presented evidence of the superior academic achievement of students in math and reading in China and Japan in comparison to their counterparts in the United States. They also distilled lessons America should learn from China and Japan to improve its education.

More convincing and systematically collected evidence came the next year. In 1995, the Third International Mathematics and Science Study (TIMSS) was conducted. With over 40 education systems participating, East Asian systems took the top spots. In both 4th- and 8th-grade math, Singapore, South Korea, Japan, and Hong Kong were the top four. Although their performance in science was not as stunning, Korea and Japan ranked first and second, respectively, in 4th-grade science, and Singapore, Japan, and Korea were first, third, and fourth, respectively, in 8th-grade science. The East Asian systems maintained their superiority in the 2003 TIMSS, which was renamed Trends in International Mathematics and Science Study, keeping the same acronym. Singapore, Hong Kong, Korea, Japan, and Taiwan were all top performers in math and science. Later cycles of TIMSS in 2007, 2011, and 2015 continued to show that students in East Asian education systems had the best performance (Mullis et al., 1997; Mullis, Martin, & Foy, 2008; Mullis, Martin, Foy, & Arora, 2012; Mullis, Martin, & Loveless, 2016; National Center for Education Statistics, 1999).

Results of PISA corroborated the finding that East Asian education systems are superior. PISA is coordinated by the Paris-based OECD. First administered in 2000, PISA typically focuses on the performance of 15-year-olds in math, reading, and science, with occasional inclusion of other domains such as problem solving. Given every 3 years since 2000, PISA has become the world's largest international educational assessment, with some 70 countries participating in the 2015 round. East Asian education systems have always been the top performers in the rounds of PISA administered in 2000, 2003, 2006, 2009, 2012, and 2015. For example, in the most recent round, the top seven educations systems in math performance were from East Asia, namely, Singapore, Hong Kong, Macau, Taiwan, Japan, China, and South Korea. Seven out of the top 10 performers in science were East Asian: Singapore, Japan, Taiwan, Macau, Vietnam, Hong Kong, and China (OECD, 2011, 2014, 2016; PISA, 2003, 2007).

While PISA affirmed the status of East Asian education systems as the best in the world, it particularly brought China into the spotlight. Mainland China participated in the 2009 round of PISA. This was the first time it participated in any large-scale international assessments. More important, students from China, represented by its most developed city, Shanghai, outperformed everyone in the world in all three domains. They did the same in 2012. In 2015, Chinese participation expanded beyond Shanghai to include Beijing, Jiangsu, and Zhejiang. Chinese students' performance in science and math was as stunning as before, although the country was no longer number one.

The PISA results officially earned China the title of the world's best education system, and that victory had a powerful effect on the West. *The New York Times* reported that the Chinese students' performance had "stunned" American experts and political leaders (Dillion, 2010). "An absolute wake-up call" to U.S. Secretary of Education Arne Duncan, it gave President Obama another "Sputnik moment," suggesting that China had beaten America in education just as the former Soviet Union beat America into space. BBC reporter Sean Coughlan wrote an article titled "China: The World's Cleverest Country?" in reaction to China's PISA performance. In the article, he summed up PISA director Schleicher's praise for Chinese education: Not only would the test results for disadvantaged pupils be the envy of any Western country, but taken as a whole, "the findings indicate that China has an education system that is overtaking many Western countries" (Coughlan, 2012).

Policymakers in the West are convinced that East Asia is superior and holds the medicine for the ills that have plagued education in the West. For example, in December 2010, shortly after visiting China and Singapore, British Secretary of Education Michael Gove published a passionate commentary in *The Telegraph*. He recounted his amazement when he was given a book of published research papers, all written by students in a Beijing school. "Schools in the Far East are turning out students who are working at an altogether higher level than our own," Gove (2010) wrote, urging his country "to implement a cultural revolution just like the one they've had in China." At the close of his commentary, he announced, "Like Chairman Mao, we've embarked on a Long March to reform our education system."

There are critics who question East Asia's superior performance over the years. Some question the validity and reliability of the methods employed by PISA and TIMSS (Feniger & Lefstein, 2014; Kreiner & Christensen, 2014; Morrison, 2013; Stewart, 2013); others doubt the sampling of participants (Loveless, 2014). There certainly are issues with the tests that identified East Asian education systems as the best, but they are not significant enough to discredit the superior academic achievement of those systems. In other words, if test scores are the measures of quality of education, East Asian education is indeed outstanding.

## THE ASIAN TREATMENT

This outstanding education is equally effective in producing other outcomes beside excellent performance on tests. The other outcomes are unpleasant, damaging, and unwanted. They are negative side effects that East Asian education systems have been working hard to fight against. This is why East Asians find it striking and surprising that the West looks to them for ideas to improve its education. They are perplexed by the sudden love for what they have had for a long time, a system they have been working to overhaul (J. Kim & Kim, 2014; Zhao, 2015a; Zhao & Wang, 2018).

> East Asians find it striking and surprising that the West looks to them for ideas to improve its education.

Admirers of East Asian education have been working hard to find the secrets that lead to its success. Critics of East Asian education have been working equally hard to identify the culprit that leads to its failure. Ironically, they are the same.

### Valuing Education

One generally agreed-upon reason for the success of East Asian students is that the East Asian cultures place a high value on education. "There is a high value placed on education and a belief that effort rather than innate ability is the key to success," wrote Mark Boylan for the *Business Insider* in 2016. "East Asian researchers usually point to this as the most important factor for this [region's] high test results," added Boylan, a professor of education at UK's Sheffield Institute of Education and the leader of the longitudinal evaluation of Britain's experiment with importing teachers and teaching from China's Shanghai.

Others agree. "For centuries, Chinese people have believed in the value of education for the nation's well-being as well as for their own personal advancement," wrote Harold Stevenson and his team of researchers at the University of Michigan more than 20 years ago (Chen, Lee, & Stevenson, 1996, p. 83). The PISA team reached a similar conclusion: "China has a long tradition of valuing education highly" (OECD, 2011, p. 86). *New York Times* columnist Nicholas Kristof (2011) noted that "the greatest strength of the Chinese system is the Confucian reverence for education that is steeped into the culture." East Asian cultures have all been influenced by Confucianism; thus, the Confucian reverence for education is shared across the region's education systems.

## Devoted Parents

The high value placed on education in East Asia leads to a high level of parental devotion to their children's education, which is another factor contributing to Asian students' academic achievement. Parents devote tremendous amounts of financial resources to their children's education. Family education expenditure in China is almost equal to if not more than the amount invested by government at the compulsory education stage, which is supposedly free (Tu & Lin, 2009). In 2015, nearly half of Chinese families, most of whom had one child, spent over 6,000RMB (about U.S. $1,000) on their children's education and 30% spent over 10,000RMB (J. Wu, 2015). The amount is significant, considering the average urban household income was about 31,000RMB in 2015. In Korea, too, education spending by families almost matches that of the government, with a ratio of 0.8 to 1 (Southgate, 2009). East Asian parents spent a much larger proportion of their income on children's education than parents in the West (HSBC, 2017).

Devoted East Asian parents are much more likely to send their children to private tutoring outside school. In Hong Kong, over 85% of secondary students receive private tutoring (Bray & Lykins, 2012). In Singapore, families spent about S$820 million on private tutoring in 2008 (Bray & Lykins, 2012). A more recent survey conducted by the global bank HSBC in 2017 found that 93% of parents in Mainland China, 88% in Hong Kong, 82% in Singapore, and 75% in Taiwan were paying for private tutoring, while the global average was 63%. The percentage in the United States was 46%, in Canada 31%, in Australia 30%, and in the UK only 23% (HSBC, 2017).

East Asian parents are also more likely than others to make personal sacrifices for their children's education. The same HSBC survey found that parents in Hong Kong, Taiwan, and Mainland China are the most likely to have reduced or completely stopped leisure activities/holidays. The survey also found that parents in Hong Kong, Malaysia, and Indonesia are the most likely to have given up "me time" (defined as personal time for parents) for their children's education (HSBC, 2017).

## Hardworking Students

Parents can support, but the work has to be done by the children. Students' intensive engagement with schoolwork is the hallmark of East Asian education and the direct contributor to their superb performance. Supported, motivated, or coerced, East Asian students work the hardest on school-related tasks. They generally spend a lot more time in schools than their peers in the West. In Japan, for example, "students have the equivalent of several more years of schooling by the time they finish high school than, say, the typical American student," according to an OECD report (2011, p. 144). The school time comes from short summer vacations and longer school weeks and days. Students in other East Asian systems have similar experiences.

In addition to time in school, East Asian students also spent more time on homework. For example, students in Shanghai spent twice as much time on homework as the OECD average (13.7 hours vs. 7 hours) and 2.5 times the OECD average on academic studies outside school (17 hours vs. 7.8 hours) per week. The same is true for students in other places in China. "Students in China's primary and secondary schools spend an average of three hours poring over homework assignments every day, twice the global average," reported the Chinese English newspaper *China Daily* in 2015 (Jing, 2015).

## Centralized and Standardized Curriculum

Another important contributor to East Asia's excellent showing in international tests is centralized and standardized curriculum. All East Asian systems have a carefully prescribed curriculum framework. This curriculum is centralized and mandated for all students. The curriculum is also very detailed, prescribing what is to be learned at any given point. Moreover, the curriculum is enforced through testing.

Marc Tucker, CEO of the National Center for Education and the Economy, wrote about the contribution of centralized and standardized curriculum to student performance, after examining several top PISA performers, in his book *Surpassing Shanghai: An Agenda for American Education Built on the World's Leading Systems*:

> These countries work out a curriculum framework, which means they decide, as a matter of policy, what topics should be taught at each grade level in each of the subjects in the curriculum. In this way, they make sure that each year the students are taking the material that will be prerequisite to the study of the material they are supposed to master the following year and that all students will be ready for advanced material when it is offered. Further, in these countries, the materials prepared by textbook publishers and publishers of supplementary materials are aligned with the national curriculum framework.
>
> Thus, the standards are aligned with the curriculum, which is aligned with the instructional materials available to teachers. And the examinations are also aligned with the curriculum, as is the training that prospective teachers get in teacher training institutions. (Tucker, 2011, p. 175)

## High-Stakes Testing

High-stakes testing is commonplace in East Asian education systems. Technically, the only high-stakes test is the college entrance exam, which decides children's future by determining which tiers of college they can attend. But this one high-stakes test has a trickle-down effect on lower grades, which are pressured to use high-stakes tests of their own. The rank and reputation of a college have direct impact on what kinds of jobs its graduates may be able to get. Since some high schools are better than others at preparing students for the college entrance exam, parents, teachers, and students in middle schools work hard to pass exams to get into these high schools. And since some middle schools are better at getting their students into better high schools, it is only natural that students in elementary school work hard so they can pass tests to get into better middle schools. For the same reason, kindergartners work hard to pass exams to better elementary schools. And of course, better kindergartens use various forms of tests to select children.

In this sense, all exams are high-stakes exams. They serve as gateways to better education opportunities. Thus, it is no exaggeration that the East Asian education system exists to prepare children for exams. Noting that all high-performing systems in PISA have a system of gateways and checkpoints—that is, tests and exams—Marc Tucker (2011) best explains the benefits of test-oriented education:

*It is no exaggeration that the East Asian education system exists to prepare children for exams.*

> In countries with gateway exam systems of this sort, every student has a very strong incentive to take tough courses and to work hard in school. A student who does not do that will not earn the credentials needed to achieve her dream, whether that dream is becoming a brain surgeon or an auto mechanic. Because the exams are scored externally, the student knows that the only way to move on is to meet the standard. Because they are national or provincial standards, the exams cannot be gamed. Because the exams are of a very high quality, they cannot be "test prepped"; the only way to succeed on them is to actually master the material. And because the right parties were involved in creating the exams, students know that the credentials they earn will be honored; when their high schools say they are "college and career ready," colleges and employees will agree. (pp. 174–175)

*"Because the exams are of a very high quality, they cannot be 'test prepped'; the only way to succeed on them is to actually master the material."*

## Manufactured Scarcity and Hierarchical Organization

While the aforementioned ingredients of East Asian education that contribute to the high performance of its stu-
dents have been mentioned often, the most
important one is not discussed commonly.
This ingredient is the one that sets everything
in motion. Without this ingredient, parents
would not value education as much, nor
would they invest as much. Likewise, without this ingredient, students would not be as
hardworking, and no centralized and standardized curriculum or system of testing would be devised.

> This ingredient . . . that sets everything in motion . . . is a legacy from the thousands of years of Confucianism and the Imperial Exam: the manufactured scarcity of desirable opportunities.

This ingredient is a legacy from the thousands of years of Confucianism
and the Imperial Exam: the manufactured scarcity of desirable opportunities and the mechanism to distribute them (Cheng, 2011; Zhao, 2014). The
Confucian tradition convinced people that there is only one type of position
worth pursuing and the only way to achieve the position is through passing
exams. For thousands of years, government positions have been promoted
as the only jobs worth pursuing in China and other places influenced by
Confucian thinking, because they have been associated with not only power
and material wealth but also social status. Although today the variety of
rewarding jobs has expanded drastically, the belief that there are only a
limited number of professions worth pursuing continues.

The supply of positions in any one profession is limited; thus, if everyone decides to pursue the same jobs, the natural outcome is fierce competition. The competition is made fiercer by the concept of hierarchy rooted
in Confucian cultures. While every society is organized in a pyramid-like
hierarchy, with fewer people above more people in terms of power and
wealth, in the Confucian cultures hierarchical thinking is much more pervasive and psychologically powerful. First, hierarchy is used to distribute
everything from power and income to the location of one's seat at a dinner
table. Second, the pervasiveness and long history of hierarchical thinking
have convinced people that there is no intrinsically valuable position. Since
there is always the next level to reach, one's self-worth is based on reaching
the next level. Being good means being better than others.

The concept of hierarchy and ranking is so rampant in East Asia that
whenever a choice needs to be made about anything, people want to know
whether it is top-ranked. This applies to fashion brands, restaurants, tourist
spots, jobs, and of course schools. Thus, it is not enough simply to enter the right profession; one then must climb to the top in order to show

accomplishment. As a result, everyone is in constant competition for fewer positions at the next level, making the competition fiercer and unrelenting.

The Imperial Exam tradition has another legacy that is at work. The Imperial Exam system was considered a transparent, fair, and objective way to award powerful and lucrative positions. It was a meritocracy (Young, 1958). It gave everyone hope because it seemed that everyone and anyone, regardless of their background or ability, could achieve the powerful positions as long as they could pass the exams. It was believed that passing the exams required only studying hard. Thus, in East Asian countries, there is a pervasive belief that effort is more important than ability (Cheng, 2011; Stevenson & Stigler, 1994).

Viewing education as the only way, "the sole path for upwards social mobility, the only hope for an individual's future" (Cheng, 2011, p. 24), mobilizes, incentivizes, or pressures parents and students to devote everything to education. But education has a special meaning in the East Asian context. It means preparation for passing exams. Because of the manufactured scarcity of good positions, good schools, and good universities, and the hierarchical thinking, education becomes a fierce competition, in which the students, parents, and teachers constantly are working to outperform others, resulting in very hardworking students, parents, and teachers (Cheng, 2011; Zhao, 2014).

## ASIAN TREATMENT AT WORK: EFFECTS AND SIDE EFFECTS

The mixture of these ingredients makes an extremely effective treatment for test scores in a limited number of areas. It sets clear goals. Everyone—students, teachers, and parents—understands what matters, which is to score high on high-stakes exams. Everyone puts all their resources into, and works hard toward, achieving these goals. They do not allow anything else to distract the students from working for these goals. The only job for the children is to secure good test scores—they are freed from any household chores or other responsibilities; they are not allowed to engage in extracurricular activities such as sports, video games, or hanging out that don't contribute to test scores. Moreover, they are not even allowed to read books that are not believed to contribute directly to test scores.

> The only job for the children is to secure good test scores—they are freed from any . . . chores or . . . responsibilities; . . . not allowed . . . extracurricular activities . . . not even allowed to read books that are not believed to contribute directly to test scores.

They work only on passing the exams and only on exams of subjects that matter, which typically include native language, math, English, and science. They don't waste time on other subjects if they are not counted as part of admission to colleges. Because it is passing the exams that ultimately matters, they don't even care about content and skills in specific subjects if the content and skills are not assessed on the exams. Furthermore, scoring high on tests is about finding the correct answers demanded by the test-makers. Thus, students and teachers focus on finding the answers without wasting energy on exploring knowledge beyond the answers. Students also spend time learning about test-taking skills.

As a result, East Asian students spend more time studying fewer subjects than their Western peers. They are not distracted by their own interests or hobbies, nor do they bother with actual understanding of the materials as long as they can give back the correct answers. They also are taught by teachers skilled in and devoted to test prepping, both outside and inside schools. It actually would be surprising if the East Asian students had not done as well as they did in international tests such as TIMSS and PISA, which have tested only math, science, and reading.

The effects of the Asian educational treatment are well supported by evidence gathered from TIMSS and PISA. However, this potent Asian treatment is also effective in causing other outcomes, most of which are undesirable and unwanted. Although these side effects have not been systematically studied through randomized controlled experiments, there is sufficient evidence of their existence. The East Asians have long criticized and sought to overhaul their own education because of its damages. The damages are essentially the adverse side effects of the same treatment that is effective in achieving excellent test scores.

## Loss of Confidence and Interest

East Asia's students have ranked among the lowest in terms of their reported confidence in mathematics, despite their top performance in test scores (Ho, 2003; Leung, 2002; Zhao, 2016a, 2016b, 2016c, 2016d). In the 1995 TIMSS results, for example, the percentages of students reporting themselves as "very confident" in math and science in 1995 in East Asian systems were much lower than in Australia, the UK, and the United States. Historically, East Asian students consistently have reported lower confidence in math than U.S. students, who have consistently scored much lower in TIMSS mathematics.

PISA has shown similar patterns. In the 2012 PISA study, students in East Asian systems reported the lowest self-confidence in the world (OECD,

2013). A high proportion of students in these education systems worried that they "will get poor grades in mathematics." More than 70% of students in Korea, Chinese Taipei, Singapore, Vietnam, Shanghai–China, and Hong Kong–China—in contrast to less than 50% in Austria, the United States, Germany, Denmark, Sweden, and the Netherlands—"agreed" or "strongly agreed" that they worried about getting poor grades in math (OECD, 2013).

East Asian students also have ranked low in their attitudes toward the tested subjects: math, reading, and science. They tend to like the subjects less and value them less than students in other countries. Moreover, while their performance on tests has continued to improve over the years, their confidence and attitudes have not. Instead, they seem to have declined (Zhao, 2016a, 2016b, 2016c, 2016d).

These findings seem counterintuitive because it is more reasonable to expect high performance to make the students more confident and more interested in the subjects. This is in fact the case within education systems. For example, TIMSS has reported positive correlations between test scores and confidence as well as attitude *within* individual education systems (Loveless, 2006a). In other words, at the individual level, students who scored higher tend to be more confident within education systems.

Thus, the fact that East Asian students have low confidence could be an effect of the system. These systems have a small percentage of students who have confidence in their math. That does not necessarily mean that high-performing students within these systems have low confidence, or vice versa. Rather, it means that these systems have somehow made a large proportion of students lose confidence and interest in math, science, and reading, while helping them achieve excellence in testing.

It is therefore not unreasonable to hypothesize that these education systems may be effective in preparing students to achieve excellent scores *and* effective in lowering their confidence and interest. They help with improving test scores but hinder the development of confidence and interest.

The Asian treatment has at least three mechanisms that could cause a loss of confidence and intrinsic interest. First, hierarchical thinking and the practice of ranking can make students feel they are never good enough because there is always someone who is better. Second, the focus on passing exams detracts from the enjoyment and the intrinsic value of the studied subjects. Third, focusing only on test scores can make students who are not good at taking tests, and may be excellent otherwise, less confident and interested in the subject because

*The focus on passing exams detracts from the enjoyment and the intrinsic value of the studied subjects.*

there is no way to acknowledge their excellence if it is not demonstrated through test scores.

These are hypotheses that have not been confirmed with large-scale and longitudinal studies, but there is preliminary evidence. One piece of evidence is the negative correlation between students' confidence and test scores across education systems. In the 2003 TIMSS, math scores and confidence in the subject were significantly negatively correlated, in both 4th and 8th grades ($r = -.59$ and $r = -.64$, respectively) (Loveless, 2006a). The correlation between nations' average scores and enjoyment is also negative ($r = -0.67$ for 4th grade and $r = -0.76$ for 8th grade). Similar negative relationships exist between PISA scores and students' noncognitive qualities. "It seems that pupils in high-scoring countries also develop the most negative attitudes to the subject" (Sjøberg, 2012, p. 1). There is also a significant negative correlation between students' self-efficacy in science and their scores in the subject across education systems in the 2015 PISA results, for example (OECD, 2016). Additionally, PISA scores have been found to have a significant negative correlation with entrepreneurial confidence and intentions (Zhao, 2012a).

The lack of confidence has caused grave concerns in East Asian education systems. After publication of the 2011 TIMSS results, the Singapore Ministry of Education (2012) noted: "Despite performing better, our students expressed less confidence in these subject areas than their peers in other education systems." The consistent expression of low confidence and interest of Korean students "suggest that it is an important . . . goal for educators in Korea to turn their attention to the affective aspects of education" (K. Kim, 2010, p. 274) because "affective variables are not only important in subject learning but are significant in themselves" (p. 280).

Hong Kong had similar reactions to its students' lack of confidence and interest in the subjects where they earned high scores on international assessments. For instance, Frederick Leung, a professor at Hong Kong University, which coordinated TIMSS in the region, said that while Hong Kong students are good at "earning high scores," the lack of interest is of concern. "Students are expected to meet the expectations of their parents and society," Leung told *The Standard*, a local newspaper. "However, interest is very important because we are now talking about lifelong learning. Without interest, students will turn away from learning once there are no longer exams" (Li, 2013).

### Loss of Well-Being—Myopia, Anxiety, Depression, and Suicide

Another potential side effect related to the loss of confidence is damage to the general physical, social, and psychological well-being of students in

East Asian countries. It is no secret that students in East Asia experience a tremendous amount of pressure and a lack of time and opportunities to engage in other activities for physical and social well-being. The impact on children's health and social and psychological well-being has been observed and reported frequently (Carey, 2015; Jiang, 2010; Zhao, 2009).

East Asian children, for example, are less healthy than their Western counterparts. For example, they have a much higher rate of myopia. A study found that up to 90% of Asian children, including those in China, Taiwan, Japan, Singapore, and Korea, are nearsighted, while the overall rate of myopia in Britain is less than 30% (Carey, 2015). Psychologically, they suffer from high anxiety, frequent suicidal thoughts, and depression (Carey, 2015; Jiang, 2010; Zhao, 2009). A 2009 study found that 24% of students in Shanghai had thought about killing themselves (Carey, 2015). A *China Daily* article ("Suicide the Leading Cause," 2007) reported results of a 2-year study by researchers at Peking University, which found that 20.4% of high school students said they had considered killing themselves at some point. The percentage was 13% for all students (elementary and secondary) in Zhejiang Province, one of coastal China's more developed areas, according to a separate study (Huicong Net, 2005).

*24% of students in Shanghai had thought about killing themselves*

Students in East Asia are generally less happy than their peers in other parts of the world. In 2017, OECD released a report on students' well-being in the more than 70 education systems that participated in the 2015 cycle of PISA. According to the report, students in East Asian education systems are significantly less "satisfied with life" than children in the West. The average scores for life satisfaction of students in China (6.83), Korea (6.36), Japan (6.80), Hong Kong (6.48), Macau (6.59), and Chinese Taipei (6.59) are all significantly below the OECD average of 7.31. No data were reported for Singapore and Vietnam, the other two East Asian education systems that participated in the PISA study. By comparison, the life satisfaction score for the United States was 7.36, the Netherlands 7.83, and Finland 7.89.

East Asian students also reported significantly higher levels of schoolwork-related anxiety than the average student measured in the 2015 PISA. With the average being 0, the schoolwork-related anxiety index for China was 0.2, Japan 0.3, Korea 0.1, Hong Kong 0.3, Macau 0.4, and Chinese Taipei 0.4. Singaporean students were the most anxious, with an anxiety index of 0.6 (OECD, 2017).

East Asian students also reported a significantly lower sense of belonging in schools. The PISA report shows that Macau, Hong Kong, China, and Singapore ranked among the lowest in terms of sense of belonging. In contrast, students in Spain, Austria, Switzerland, and Germany reported a very high sense of belonging in schools (OECD, 2017).

## Loss of Talent Diversity

The Asian education treatment has another, less reported side effect. It can result in a loss of diversity of human talents. There is no direct experimental evidence of this side effect so far because of the lack of tradition of attending to side effects in education. However, there is strong historical and macro-level data to draw upon. The history of China's failure to be the first to modernize is an excellent case.

Before the Industrial Revolution, China was by far the most advanced and most prosperous country in the world. China far outpaced other nations in technological innovations until the Industrial Revolution, as convincingly documented in the 24-volume series *Science and Civilisation in China* authored by Cambridge University sinologist Joseph Needham (Needham, 1954).

"Most scholars believe that, as early as in the early period of Ming Dynasty (14th century), China had acquired all the major elements that were essential for the British industrial revolution in the 18th century," asserts Justin Yifu Lin (2006, p. 5), a former vice president of the World Bank and professor of economics at China's Peking University. In other words, China was almost ready for the Industrial Revolution—400 years before Great Britain was. "However, the industrial revolution occurred in Britain instead of China and Chinese economy was quickly overtaken and lagged behind by western countries" (J. Y. Lin, 2006, p. 5).

But why did the Industrial Revolution not start in China, the nation that first acquired all the major conditions? Many scholars asked similar questions: "Why had China been so far in advance of other civilizations?" and "Why is China not now ahead of the rest of world?" (J. Y. Lin, 2006).

The Imperial Exam or *keju,* the invention that helped China to become a powerful and technologically advanced empire in ancient times, was also the reason for China's failure to start the Industrial Revolution (Zhao, 2014). After methodically examining a number of existing hypotheses that attribute the lack of scientific revolution in China to economic reasons (land to people ratio or a repressive political environment), J. Y. Lin (2006) found *keju* to be the real culprit:

> Because of this examination system, curious geniuses were diverted from learning mathematics and conducting controllable experiments. Because of this system,

the geniuses could not accumulate crucial human capital that was essential for the scientific revolution. As a result, the discoveries of natural phenomena could only be based on sporadic observations, and could not be upgraded into modern science, which was built upon mathematics and controlled experiments. (pp. 12–13)

Essentially, what prevented China from initiating the innovations that led to a new age for humanity was the side effect of its great invention, the *keju* (Zhao, 2014). The *keju* was a powerful intervention that was extremely effective in homogenizing the population and instilling compliance, which sustained a great agricultural empire. An agricultural society that sought stability needed a homogeneous and compliant citizenry that did not wish to deviate from or challenge authority. But scientific discoveries and technological innovations require a diversity of talented people who are willing to deviate and challenge existing orders.

The modern-day Asian treatment, the education arrangement that the West admires and wishes to borrow, has the same effects. The mechanisms that lead to the excellent scores on PISA and TIMSS also lead to a reduction of talent diversity. Humans are born with different talents and needs, and these innate differences interact with their experiences and create a diversity of unique jagged profiles of abilities and interests (Gardner, 1983, 1993; Reiss, 2004, 2008; Ridley, 2003; Rose, 2016; Sternberg, 1988; Zhao, 2018). This diversity can be greatly reduced in a number of ways in an education system that values homogeneity.

First, the centralized and standardized curriculum limits students' exposure to only knowledge and skills included in the curriculum, thus depriving children of opportunities to discover their natural talents and interests. As a Hong Kong University education professor observed about students in Shanghai: "They have little direct encounter with nature, for example, and little experience with the society in general" (Cheng, 2011, p. 34). As a result, many children do not even know what they are good at or interested in, which has become a frequently reported problem in East Asia—many students do not know their strengths or passion and thus do not know what to study in college. Even if by accident a child discovers his or her strength, the strictly enforced curriculum provides no room for the child to develop that strength or interest further.

Second, the frequent exams—the gateways and checkpoints Marc Tucker (2011) praises as effective systemic features for high performance—ensure that students do not explore anything beyond what's being tested. Parents and teachers are there to make sure that their students do not waste time studying things not covered in the tests because of the stakes the tests carry. More important, these exams recognize individuals talented only in the tested subjects and in test-taking. Individuals who are talented in other areas or are uninterested in studying the prescribed subjects are suppressed by or eliminated from the system (Zhao, 2009, 2014, 2015b, 2018).

Third, teachers, who are well trained to strictly follow the centralized and standardized curriculum, teach at the same pace, following the same sequence and using the same textbooks for all students. There is very little room for exploring individual interests and accommodating different learning styles. Moreover, teachers, in the pursuit of high test scores, not only discourage students from exploring interests that do not contribute to high test scores but also actively suppress their pursuit of knowledge other than what's tested, by overwhelming them with homework and test preparation (Zhao, 2009, 2018).

Finally, students receiving the Asian treatment are likely to engage in self-censorship. In order to please (or for fear of angering) their parents and teachers, children who may be talented and interested in domains other than the prescribed subjects have to conceal, suppress, or outright give up their talents or interests. Their parents or teachers may comfort them by telling them that they can pursue their own interests and talents after passing the college entrance exam, but for some that may be too late because by then they may have lost the interest or the opportunity to develop their talents.

*In order to please (or for fear of angering) their parents and teachers, children who may be talented and interested in domains other than the prescribed subjects have to conceal, suppress, or outright give up their talents or interests.*

The effectiveness of East Asian education in reducing talent diversity comes from its intent to homogenize. The more successful the education system is at homogenizing, the higher test scores it achieves, and, at the same time, the more effective it is at eliminating diversity. This is why Kim and Kim said Albert Einstein could not survive the Korean education system and would not be admitted to prestigious universities in Korea, and could not find a job at Samsung, which hires only graduates from prestigious universities (J. Kim & Kim, 2014). This is also why Steve Jobs would not have become Steve Jobs had he been born in China (Zhao, 2012a) and why Steve Wozniak, co-founder of Apple with Steve Jobs, said in a 2011 interview on BBC that Apple could not have been developed in Singapore.

### Suppression and Loss of Creativity

In addition to eliminating and suppressing diversity of talents, the East Asian education system is effective in suppressing creativity, a universally pursued asset today (Florida, 2002, 2012; Zhao, 2015b). But here again we face the problem of lacking direct experimental evidence from longitudinal studies to establish causality between the Asian education system and creativity. But based on historical evidence and studies on the development or loss of creativity, we can reasonably suspect the negative effect of East Asian education on creativity.

The lack of creativity in East Asia is a generally recognized problem both in and outside the region (Barber, Donnelly, & Rizvi, 2012; K. H. Kim, 2005; Zhao, 2009, 2014). Although East Asian countries have risen to global prominence as economic powers, their economic success has been built on the creativity of products from the West. The miraculous economic growth in East Asia over the past few decades was driven largely by scientific discoveries and technological innovations made outside the region (Hannas, 2003). Whether East Asia will lead in creativity in the future remains debatable, but it is true that the education that produced the outstanding showing in PISA and TIMSS did not seem to lead to the same level of creativity. In fact, there is strong reason to believe it actively suppresses creativity in a number of ways.

First, creativity is not simply a cognitive process. It has a lot to do with noncognitive skills (Zhao, 2012a). Confidence, resilience, grit, mindset, personality traits, social skills, and motivation have been found to be *at least* as important as cognitive skills in the workplace (Brunello & Schlotter, 2010; Levin, 2012). The East Asian education systems compel students to spend all their time preparing for the examinations and give them almost no time to cultivate noncognitive skills and traits.

Second, examinations reward the ability to find the correct answers and give those answers in expected ways. To obtain good scores, students need to learn to guess what the examiner wants and provide answers that please the examiner. In other words, good scores are the results of giving correct answers in correct ways. Getting good scores is to comply with authority. Finding and delivering predetermined answers are antithetical to creativity, which requires the ability to come up with new solutions and pose questions that have not been asked before. As a result, East Asian students are extremely good at well-defined problems. As long as they know what they need to do to meet expectations, and they have examples to follow, they do great. But in less structured situations, without routines and formulas to fall back on, they have great difficulty. In other words, they are good at solving existing problems in predictable ways, but not at coming up with radical new solutions or inventing new problems to solve.

Third, East Asian education systems replace students' intrinsic motivation with extrinsic, utilitarian motivation. Instead of caring about what they learn, they care about what they can get by demonstrating to the authority that they have learned what the authority wants them to learn. Getting the credential is more important than actually learning—which explains why cheating on exams is rampant (Cheng, 2011; Zhao, 2014). While it is actually possible to drill basic skills and knowledge into students without them being the least bit interested in or passionate about the subject, it is impossible to force those students to be creative or seek greatness if they have neither the interest nor the passion to do so.

Finally, creativity research evidence suggests that teaching practices play a significant role in nurturing or stifling creativity (Beghetto & Kaufman, 2010; Gajda, Beghetto, & Karwowski, 2017). For example, a study of teacher behaviors and creativity found that extended and exploratory interactions between students and teachers and among students facilitated the development of creativity, while directive and rapidly closing patterns of interactions tended to stifle creativity (Gajda et al., 2017). Quickly discarding students' novel ideas and failure to explore students' ideas contribute to the "soft killing" of students' creativity (Beghetto, 2013). East Asian classrooms, in the pursuit of good testing results, often involve more direct teaching, which is more effective in instilling knowledge, as direct instruction research has shown, and in discarding students' novel ideas because they distract from mastering what needs to be mastered.

*Discarding students' novel ideas and failure to explore students' ideas contribute to the "soft killing" of students' creativity.*

## SUMMARY

The East Asian systems are indeed very effective in producing outstanding test results in a limited number of subjects. The outstanding performances on tests are accompanied by less confidence, less satisfaction, less creativity, and less diversity of talents. We have preliminary evidence and good reason to believe that these are the effects and side effects of the Asian treatment, the two sides of the same coin. Thus, policymakers and practitioners need to seriously consider whether the effects outweigh the side effects.

# CHAPTER 5

# The Rabbit Hole of Visible Learning

## Invisible Side Effects Lurk Ahead

"It is perhaps education's equivalent to the search for the Holy Grail—or the answer to life, the universe and everything," reported Warwick Mansell in the 100-year-old, UK-based education magazine *Times Education Supplement*, or *TES*, in 2008. "Grappled with by teachers and educationists for millennia, the perennial question goes a bit like this: if you could change one thing about the way our schooling system is run, what would it be?" continued Mansell. "Now, what is believed to be the largest ever educational research study—covering more than 80 million pupils and bringing together more than 50,000 smaller studies—has come up with the answer."

The Holy Grail of teaching that Mansell wrote about is a book called *Visible Learning: A Synthesis of over 800 Meta-Analyses Relating to Achievement*, authored by John Hattie (2008), an education professor at the University of Auckland in New Zealand at the time. The book reports results of Hattie's synthesis of more than 800 meta-analyses of studies related to student achievement. Although Hattie stated in the book that he wanted to give "an explanatory story, not a 'what works' recipe" (p. 3), the book turns out, or at least is perceived by many readers, to be a list of what works or what works best in education (Bergeron, 2017).

Basically, Hattie conducted a meta-analysis of other meta-analytical studies, a meta-meta-analysis in a sense. A meta-analysis is essentially a statistical approach to combining the results of many studies. It has been used in many fields as a way to come to some common truth that all existing scientific evidence supports. Hattie's synthesis resulted in a list of more than 130 influences that affect student achievement. He calculated the effect sizes for each and found that the average effect size of all interventions was 0.4; he used this "hinge point" to judge the effectiveness of the influences. He rank-ordered the influences according to their effective sizes, resulting in a list of what works best or better in education.

Hattie continued his line of work and published his updated findings in his 2012 book *Visible Learning for Teachers: Maximizing Impact on Learning* and his article "The Applicability of Visible Learning to Higher Education" (2015). The list of factors was expanded from the original 138 to 150 and then to 195 in his 2015 article. Hattie arranged the factors into six areas: the student, the home, the school, the curricula, the teacher, and teaching and learning approaches. But since he was not interested in "what cannot be influenced in schools" (Hattie, 2008, p. viii), his book is about what schools and teachers can do to help students learn.

Out of the six areas examined by Hattie, the teacher has the greatest effect. The three most effective factors are (1) self-reported grades, (2) Piagetian programs, and (3) providing formative evaluation. The factors that have weak effects are (1) multi-grade/age classes, (2) student control over learning, and (3) open versus traditional teaching. The ones that show the most negative and disabling effects are (1) retention, (2) television, and (3) familial mobility (relocation). Interested readers can check out the list of influences and their effect sizes at the Visible Learning website (visible-learning.org/nvd3/visualize/hattie-ranking-interactive-2009-2011-2015.html).

This list of influences and their effect sizes are in essence the Holy Grail of teaching, the answer to what works in teaching and learning referred to by Warwick Mansell in the 2008 *TES* article. In a field that believes in panacea, Hattie's work, with lots of numbers, simple answers to complex problems, and impressive presentations, was exactly what education policymakers, school leaders, and practitioners had been looking for. As a result, *Visible Learning* spread like wildfire globally. John Hattie and his visible learning have been embraced by policymakers and practitioners around the world. "He is not the messiah," wrote Darren Evans (2012) in *TES*, the publication that 4 years earlier had called *Visible Learning* education's Holy Grail, "but for many policy makers he comes close. John Hattie, possibly the world's most influential education academic, has the ear of governments everywhere."

Of course, Hattie and his work have not been without critics. On the contrary, Hattie as an academic and *Visible Learning* as an influential scholarly product have been criticized from different angles (Bergeron, 2017; Brown, 2013; Snook, O'Neill, Clark, O'Neill, & Openshaw, 2009; Terhart, 2011). The most serious and damaging criticism concerns the approach Hattie used to arrive at his conclusions. For example, Neil Brown, a computing education researcher at King's College London, pointed out many methodological flaws in Hattie's effect sizes. Brown (2013) charged that

Hattie's averaging and comparison of effect sizes across different studies and interventions were inappropriate, essentially confusing apples and oranges. Ewald Terhart (2011), a professor at the University of Münster in Germany, reviewed Hattie's work and concluded: "It is obvious that Hattie in fact has not found the Holy Grail of research on schooling, teaching, and teachers" (p. 436).

It gets worse. Pierre-Jérôme Bergeron, a Canadian statistician at the University of Ottawa, charged Hattie with practicing pseudoscience. In an article titled "How to Engage in Pseudoscience with Real Data: A Criticism of John Hattie's Arguments in Visible Learning from the Perspective of a Statistician," Bergeron (2017) pointed out a number of methodological errors that threaten the foundation of Hattie's conclusions. For example, Bergeron asserts: "Hattie's method is not statistically sophisticated"; "he . . . is capable of using a formula that converts a correlation into Cohen's $d$ . . . , without understanding the prerequisites for this type of conversion to be valid. He is guilty of many errors." After explaining Hattie's statistical errors in detail, Bergeron concludes: "It is clear that John Hattie and his team have neither the knowledge nor the competencies required to conduct valid statistical analyses. No one should replicate this methodology because we must never accept pseudoscience" (Bergeron, 2017).

*Serious damaging criticism concerns the approach Hattie used to arrive at his conclusions.*

*Widespread and possibly growing influence over education policies and practices around the world is cause for attention to a bigger problem: side effects.*

Whether Hattie's *Visible Learning* is education's Holy Grail or pseudoscience is certainly a very important issue to explore. But the already widespread and possibly growing influence over education policies and practices around the world is cause for attention to a bigger problem: side effects on educational outcomes besides student achievement. Hattie (2008) made it clear that his review was concerned only with student achievement, and education should have many outcomes:

*Hattie . . . made it clear that his review was concerned only with student achievement, and education should have many outcomes.*

> It is important from the start to note at least two critical codicils. Of course, there are many outcomes of schooling, such as attitudes, physical outcomes, belongingness, respect, citizenship, and the love of learning. This book focuses on student achievement, and that is a limitation of this review. (p. 6)

In other words, the effects of Hattie's list of factors, regardless of their validity, are effects on academic outcomes only. The effects on other educational outcomes were not studied. Thus, we have no idea whether the factors Hattie found to have large positive effects on achievement may negatively affect other outcomes, such as love of learning, or whether the ones Hattie found to have a negative effect on achievement actually may positively affect other outcomes, such as belongingness and citizenship.

However, policymakers and practitioners seem to have missed Hattie's disclaimer. They have equated *Visible Learning*, which is about only one outcome, with the entire education experience, which must achieve many outcomes, without any concern about the adverse side effects *Visible Learning* can have on other outcomes. But side effects are inevitable.

> *Policymakers and practitioners seem to have missed Hattie's disclaimer.*

## MANY EDUCATIONAL OUTCOMES

Schools are charged with the responsibility for cultivating qualities deemed valuable for successful functioning in a society. What is considered valuable and desirable, of course, varies a great deal across societies, but it is hard to believe that any modern society would believe that only one single quality was worth cultivating. There is no education system in the world that teaches only one subject, for example. Typically, modern schools teach a range of core subjects, such as civics, math, science, language, social sciences, and humanities. Additionally, they generally include other subjects, such as arts, music, physical education, technology/computers, economics, and so on. These academic courses include both content and skills often prescribed in some form of curriculum by a system. Schools thus are held accountable to ensure that their students master the prescribed content and skills. While schools often have been explicitly held accountable for academic outcomes, they also have been, sometimes maybe implicitly, asked to positively affect, or at least not hurt, other outcomes, such as social–emotional well-being and physical fitness.

Moreover, recent societal changes have prompted calls for schools to expand the definition of explicit educational outcomes to include the development of qualities beyond learning traditional academic content knowledge. For example, the definition of college and career readiness, a generally accepted goal for today's schools in the United States, includes five categories: (1) academic knowledge, (2) critical thinking/problem solving, (3) social and emotional learning, collaboration, and/or communication, (4) grit/resilience/perseverance, and (5) citizenship and/or community involvement

(Mishkind, 2014). The Partnership for 21st Century Skills (2007) has convinced many schools and policymakers of the importance of the 4Cs—communication, collaboration, critical thinking, and creativity. Personal qualities also have been advocated as essential (Duckworth & Yeager, 2015). Other outcomes have been suggested as well: innovation (Wagner, 2008, 2012), entrepreneurship (Aspen Institute, 2012; Zhao, 2006, 2012a), the ability to creatively respond to uncertainty (Beghetto, 2017), a growth mindset (Dweck, 2006), and social–emotional competency (Wentzel, 1991).

These are all valuable and desirable outcomes. There are compelling reasons behind all the existing and proposed knowledge, skills, abilities, attitudes, and capacities. All students should be equipped with them. But there are big questions. Can all students be equipped with them? Can they all acquire them at the same pace? Can a policy or practice lead to positive effects on all of them equally and simultaneously? This is dependent on the nature of the relationship among the many outcomes.

## AN ECOLOGICAL METAPHOR

The assumption that educational interventions can benefit and hurt, just like medical interventions, is based not only on emerging evidence but also on the logical analysis of the nature of relationships among different outcomes. Ecology provides a useful framework for understanding the relationships among the different outcomes. Ecologists have identified five important types of interactions between two organisms: (1) competition—both organisms have some kind of negative effect on each other; (2) predation—positive for one (the predator) and negative for the other (the prey); (3) parasitism—negative for one (the host) and positive for the other (the parasite); (4) commensalism—positive for one (the commensal) and no effect on the other; and (5) mutualism—positive for both (Odum, 1997).

Without pushing the ecological metaphor too far, we can imagine individual students as an ecosystem in which the different qualities interact with one another as organisms do. The different qualities (intended outcomes) can be imagined to have types of relationships similar to those of living organisms in an ecosystem. There are perhaps four types of relationships that exist among the different educational outcomes or intended qualities.

### Competition

Two outcomes compete with each other for resources. In an ecosystem, lizards and frogs are in competition because they both eat small insects.

This is a win–lose relationship. This relationship exists among educational outcomes all the time. For example, different subjects are in constant competition for time and other instructional resources, as well as students' attention. A student cannot simultaneously devote time to music and math because time is a constant. For the same reason, a school cannot possibly increase time for math or reading without taking time away from other activities. Increasing time for one subject necessarily reduces time for other subjects. As evidenced in the effect of NCLB, schools increased time for math and reading, but they had to take time away from other subjects and activities, such as social studies, science, arts, music, and even recess.

### Predation

Desired outcomes also can have a predatory relationship. In ecosystems, a predatory relationship is one in which the growth of the predator relies on the disappearance of the prey. This is also a win–lose relationship. For instance, different birds gain energy by eating earthworms, insects, or fish. A predatory relationship exists among educational outcomes because the growth of some outcomes depends on the decrease of others. For example, an increased level of obedience and compliance relies on a reduction in willingness to question the status quo and authority or to express one's own thoughts and opinions. An individual cannot be compliant and creative at the same time. Academic performance typically reflects one's willingness to follow instructions and provide predetermined answers, while creativity reflects more one's confidence and courage to question the status quo and express one's own views. Consequently, educational strategies that focus on increasing academic performance can prey on creative expression. There is evidence (e.g., Pretz & Kaufman, 2015) suggesting that high levels of academic performance in the form of high school class rank can come at the cost of creative confidence.

*A predatory relationship exists among educational outcomes because the growth of some outcomes depends on the decrease of others.*

### Commensalism

Some outcomes can benefit from other outcomes without benefiting or harming the other outcomes. The transparent shrimp that lives in a reef is an ecological example of this relationship in that the reef provides benefits to the shrimp in the form of camouflage but does not receive any benefit or damage from this relationship. This is a win–neutral relationship. In education, such relationships exist as well because the improvement in some outcomes is dependent on the increase of others but the relationship is unidirectional. For example, evidence suggests that grit and growth mindset can improve academic outcomes (Claro, Paunesku, & Dweck, 2016; Duckworth, Peterson, Matthews, & Kelly, 2007), but there is little evidence to suggest that academic outcomes increase or decrease grit or growth mindset.

## Mutualism

It is also possible for some qualities to have a relationship in which they benefit from interacting with each other. An example of this type of relationship in ecology is that of bees and flowers in which bees get nectar from flowers and in return spread pollen so the plant can reproduce. This is a win–win relationship. In education, mutually beneficial relationships exist among outcomes as well. For instance, it is possible that self-determination and emotional well-being are mutually enhancing. When one is able to experience more autonomy, he or she has an increased sense of well-being psychologically (Ryan & Deci, 2017).

The types of relationships between outcomes are simplified in Figure 5.1. Out of the four types of possible relationships, one is mutually enhancing, which means an intervention intended to improve one outcome can improve another. This is a positive side effect. One is commensalism, meaning that efforts to increase one outcome do not help or hurt the others; thus there is no side effect. Two types of relationships indicate that an intervention intended to improve one outcome can hurt the development of another, resulting in an adverse side effect.

It is apparent that an individual cannot possibly pursue all outcomes with equal levels of success, nor can a treatment result in positive effects on all outcomes. Unfortunately, the lack of attention to potential adverse side effects in education has left us with scant data to examine the effects and side effects of a treatment on different, potentially negatively

**Figure 5.1. Types of Relationships Between Two Outcomes**

|              | Outcome X | Outcome Y |
|--------------|-----------|-----------|
| Competition  | +         | –         |
| Predation    | +         | –         |
| Commensalism | +         | 0         |
| Mutualism    | +         | +         |

*If other outcomes are more important to life success, should the merit of policies and practices be judged based on their effect on other outcomes ... in addition to academic outcomes?*

related, outcomes. The majority of available evidence is about the effect or lack thereof on a single outcome. So we don't know with much certainty about adverse effects on other outcomes. This is the case with the *Visible Learning* findings, research on direct instruction, and studies of other instructional strategies and policies.

However, the analysis of the nature of relationships among different educational outcomes, supported by an emerging body of evidence, is sufficient grounds for caution on the part of policymakers, educators, and researchers. It raises important questions, such as whether the ever-expanding list of outcomes should be applied to all students or whether schools should be held accountable for achieving all the outcomes. More significant, if other outcomes are more important to life success, should the merit of policies and practices be judged based on their effect on other outcomes instead of, or at least in addition to, academic outcomes?

## OUTCOMES VERSUS OUTCOMES: SIDE EFFECTS OF PURSUING ACADEMIC ACHIEVEMENT

Academic achievement often is defined as students' mastery of the intended knowledge and skills, which frequently are prescribed in system-level curricula or standards and interpreted and implemented in the classroom. Academic achievement is subject-specific, but there are general frameworks that aim to define and classify learning goals across subjects. For example, Bloom's Taxonomy of Educational Objectives (Bloom, Englehart, Furst, Hill, & Krathwohl, 1956) and its revised version (Anderson & Sosniak, 1994; Anderson et al., 2001; Krathwohl, 2002) have been widely used to guide the development of instructional objectives across subjects, as have been Gagné's (1968) learning hierarchies and types, albeit to a lesser extent.

Academic achievement, so defined, may have predatory or competitive relationships with some other educational outcomes because the characteristics of academic achievement stand in direct contrast to some, possibly more important outcomes. Thus, efforts to improve academic achievement may lead to the decline of other, nonacademic outcomes that are perhaps more important for individuals and society. We can examine the potential side effects of interventions aimed at boosting academic achievement by analyzing the relationship between academic achievement and other outcomes.

## Homogenizing Versus Diversifying

Academic achievement is about homogenizing individuals. The highest goal for all interventions to boost academic achievement is to ensure that all students master all the intended knowledge and skills at the same rate. Consequently, the effectiveness of an intervention on academic achievement is assessed by the extent to which the intervention has succeeded in having all students master all the prescribed knowledge and skills in a given period of time. This is illustrated in the formula for computing effect size (see Figure 5.2), a favored indicator of an intervention's effectiveness. The effect size of an intervention is determined by both the level of improvement (the average difference between the treatment group and the control group) and variations among students. Put in simpler terms, if an intervention leads to very significant improvement for only some students, the average mean difference can be large but its effect size is small because of the large variation. Thus, for an intervention to be effective, it must be able to eliminate individual variations.

Educational treatments vary in terms of their scale, duration, and impact. They are not limited to a strategy to teach the multiplication table or a direct instruction program for improving reading. They also can be policies that have larger impact, such as NCLB. They also can be education systems, such as those in East Asia. Small or large, their effectiveness on academic achievement is measured in the same way: by the extent to which they are successful in homogenizing individuals. International assessments such as PISA and TIMSS judge the effectiveness of education systems by examining both the average scores and variations in content domains such as reading and math. Education systems that produce higher averages and smaller variation are considered better, more effective education systems or treatments.

## Talent Suppression

Talent suppression is perhaps one of the most serious adverse side effects of treatments to boost academic achievement. As a result of the interactions between nature and nurture (Ridley, 2003), people vary a great deal

**Figure 5.2. An Effect Size Formula**

$$\text{Effect Size} = \frac{[\text{Mean of experimental group}] - [\text{Mean of control group}]}{\text{Standard Deviation}}$$

on multiple dimensions. They are differently talented and skilled (Gardner, 1983, 1993; Sternberg, 1988), with a jagged profile of abilities in different domains (Rose, 2016). They also differ in their motivation and interests (Reiss, 2004; Zhao, 2018). They also have different personalities and mind-sets (Dweck, 1999; John, Robins, & Pervin, 2008). And, of course, their skills and knowledge in relation to a specific academic subject vary as well.

Naturally, not all students are equally talented or interested in studying the same subject, nor do they uniformly believe in the value of academic achievement. Moreover, as aptitude–treatment interaction (ATI) research suggests, not all students respond the same way to the same treatment. But interventions aimed at boosting academic achievement, by design, must be effective in having all children learn the same sub-ject equally well. Thus, the less talented, less in-terested, and less motivated students are forced to spend more time so as to improve their achievement in the desired subject or subjects. As discussed earlier, time is a constant. Those students who are willing to comply have to take time away from pursuing what they may be talented and interested in. Those who are unwilling to comply are deemed academic failures and deprived of further opportunities.

*Time is a constant.*

Furthermore, schools effective in academic achievement in a narrow set of subjects provide little chance for students who may have talent in domains outside the offered academic subjects to explore and discover their talent and interests. They might never know what they are talented and interested in. Instead, they just know what they are not good at or interested in.

Given the prominence of academic achievement in allocating opportu-nities and social resources, students who are talented in domains outside the academic subjects may not be able to seek further opportunities such as college and postgraduate studies because of their low academic perfor-mance. It is also likely, in a credential-conscious society, that they may never be given the opportunity and resources to develop their talents and pursue their interests. Consequently, these students' talents will be suppressed and their interests and passions stifled.

*Students who may have talent in domains outside the offered academic subjects . . . might never know what they are talented and interested in.*

Talent suppression happens in all educa-tion systems, but more often in systems that are extremely effective in promoting academ-ic achievement in narrower sets of subjects. As discussed in Chapter 4, East Asian education systems have experienced the most talent suppression because of their narrow definition of academic success, centralized standards, and high-stakes testing, as well as the whole apparatus that incentivizes parents, students, and teachers to pursue academic achievement.

Talent suppression is harmful for individual students. It in essence deprives children who may be talented in nonacademic ways the opportunity to reach their potential. It is also harmful to societies. Modern societies require a diversity of talent in order to prosper, and the need for talent diversity is ever-increasing as jobs that require homogenous knowledge and skills are increasingly performed by smart machines (Florida, 2012; Page, 2007; Rose, 2016; Zhao, 2015a). But talent suppression and the loss of talent diversity are an unavoidable side effect of narrow focus on academic achievement, which seeks to homogenize.

> *Talent suppression and the loss of talent diversity are an unavoidable side effect of narrow focus on academic achievement, which seeks to homogenize.*

## Short-Term Versus Long-Term

Academic achievement is often a measure of the short-term effect of interventions. Although there are measures, such as the ACT, PISA, and TIMSS, of the long-term cumulative effect of schooling in some academic domains, most of the time academic achievement is a measure of the degree to which students have mastered the intended knowledge and skills within a relatively short period of time. Grades, one of the most commonly used measures of academic achievement, typically are given at the end a course. Moreover, grades are based on even smaller units of measurement, such as weekly quizzes, the end of an instructional unit, daily homework completion, and midterm and end-of-course exams. Standardized tests often are given annually in a limited number of subjects. In research, longitudinal studies of academic achievement are not common.

Moreover, short-term academic achievement has more influence on practice and policy than long-term educational outcomes. Schools and teachers are held accountable for improving academic achievement in the short term, as exemplified by the AYP requirement in NCLB. Important decisions are made about students based on short-term academic performance. For example, students are prescribed remediation, grade retention, special education, or gifted education based on performance over a year or scores on a test. Furthermore, parents judge their children and their children's education based on improvement of academic achievement over a short period of time. Consequently, short-term academic achievement drives actions in education.

Efforts to boost short-term academic outcomes can have adverse side effects on other important, long-term outcomes. There is emerging evidence that short-term positive academic outcomes do not necessarily translate into long-term life quality outcomes. For example, the longitudinal study by Howard Friedman, mentioned in Chapter 3, found that early literacy was negatively associated with important indicators of life quality, such as social–emotional well-being and adjustment in the long term (Kern & Friedman, 2009).

There is also evidence that instructional interventions that result in more effective information acquisition or imitation can cause a suppression of curiosity and creativity in young children, as discussed in Chapter 3 (Bonawitza et al., 2011; Buchsbauma et al., 2011). Although it is unlikely that a one-time treatment of direct instruction would cause lifelong damage to creativity or curiosity, repeated direct teaching over time could (Zhao, 2014). For example, researchers have found a significantly negative relationship between academic outcomes such as high school class rank and students' confidence to generate creative ideas (Pretz & Kaufman, 2015). Researchers also have found that extracurricular activities tend to be a stronger predictor of creative expression in college applicants than traditional admissions factors, such as SAT scores and high school rank (Cotter, Pretz, & Kaufman, 2016).

The peculiar negative correlations between scores and confidence across education systems, repeatedly found in TIMSS and other international studies, provide further evidence. In TIMSS, for example, there is a consistent pattern of students in education systems with higher scores tending to show less interest, enjoyment, and confidence in the tested subjects, as discussed in Chapter 4. Similar patterns also exist in PISA (Sjøberg, 2012; Zhao, 2012a, 2012b).

In today's world, creativity, curiosity, confidence, and interest in a subject are much more significant qualities to cultivate than the achievement of short-term academic outcomes (Florida, 2012; Wagner, 2012). More important, they are more difficult to restore once lost than academic knowledge. Students can catch up academically if they are interested in the subject and have confidence that they can learn it. But if they have lost interest and confidence because of efforts to boost their short-term academic achievement, it will be much harder for them to get back their interest and confidence.

> *In today's world, creativity, curiosity, confidence, and interest in a subject are much more significant. . . . More important, they are more difficult to restore once lost than academic knowledge.*

Certain interventions that are effective in improving short-term academic outcomes also can negatively affect long-term academic outcomes. For example, research has found that teaching decoding skills does not improve reading comprehension; however, decoding skills can be viewed by some as a necessary part of reading achievement. Thus, effort and time devoted to learning decoding skills are time and effort away from actually learning to read. Some strategies that teach children to memorize facts can show immediate positive effect, but they may negatively damage children's interest in the subject or constrain them from developing deeper conceptual understanding of the subject (Kapur, 2014, 2016).

## Cognitive Versus Noncognitive

Academic outcomes are more in the cognitive than the noncognitive domain. They are more often than not about students' ability to memorize, follow directions, and apply information to solve problems. They relate to a person's ability to perform certain tasks in a certain way. They typically do not consider a person's desire to perform the tasks, which often is affected by a host of factors generally referred to as noncognitive skills. As result, very rarely are noncognitive outcomes such as motivation, persistence, confidence, and personality traits included in formal assessments of academic outcomes.

Noncognitive outcomes are not a single unit; rather, they refer to a wide range of personal qualities that are not typically or directly associated with cognitive abilities. The list of proposed noncognitive qualities is long. Some of the commonly cited ones include grit, motivation, confidence, conscientiousness, growth mindset, self-determination, self-control, emotional intelligence, social intelligence, gratitude, open-mindedness, and curiosity.

These diverse qualities have been found to enhance socioemotional well-being, facilitate goal-oriented effort, and help in making better judgments and decisions (Duckworth & Yeager, 2015). Research has confirmed that these qualities are strongly associated with economic, psychological, and physical well-being, contributing to individuals' lifelong success (Brunello & Schlotter, 2010; Duckworth & Yeager, 2015; Levin, 2012). This is why academic outcomes (e.g., test scores) alone have not been reliable predictors of the future success of individuals or nations (Baker, 2007; Goleman, 1995; Tienken, 2008; Zhao, 2016a).

Noncognitive qualities may be difficult to teach explicitly. While it is unrealistic to fashion them into specific outcomes of a single course or two, the school experience can have a significant effect on the development of noncognitive qualities, as can cultural norms, value orientation of schools and education systems, and teachers and families. An exclusive focus on improving cognitive skills, particularly under the pressure of scoring high on standardized tests, can cause damage to noncognitive qualities. For instance, while the practice of publicly ranking students based on test scores, as practiced in many schools in China, certainly can help motivate students to score better, it also can decrease students' confidence in their abilities. Except for a small group of students who are on top, the majority of students feel worse. Likewise, rote learning and direct instruction may result in short-term gains on test scores, but they can cause a loss of interest and engagement in the subjects because the teaching method inevitably makes the subjects much less interesting than they actually are.

## SUMMARY

Education has many different outcomes, all of which are worth pursuing. But given the nature of their relationships, not all of the outcomes can co-exist peacefully in a mutually beneficial way in one person. Efforts that have a positive effect on one outcome may have an adverse side effect on another. Therefore, promoting or discarding educational interventions or treatments based simply on their effects on academic outcomes is not wise. For example, John Hattie's reviews show that direct instruction has an effect size of 0.60, well above his hinge point of 0.4, and thus it is an effective influence on student achievement. However, as discussed in Chapter 3, direct instruction has a negative effect on creativity and curiosity. In contrast, Hattie found the effect size of "student control of learning" to be only 0.01, which means it has no effect on student achievement and should not be used. However, "student control of learning" may benefit students in the long term and have a positive effect on their confidence, sense of autonomy, and self-determination.

There is no Holy Grail in education. The effects of educational treatments vary because of the individual variability of students. They can be positive for some students, but detrimental to others. They also differ because of variations in outcomes. They can be effective in improving some outcomes, but can be equally effective in impeding the development of others.

# CHAPTER 6

# From When Is It Effective to Who Gets Hurt

## When Vouchers Don't Work

"Our results indicate that a general increase in teacher cognitive abilities would increase the achievement gap between high and low-performing students, both by raising the achievement of high-performing students and lowering it for low-performing ones," write Erik Gronqvist and Jonas Vlachos (2008, p. 27), researchers at the Swedish Research Institute of Industrial Economics, summarizing their findings from a study that examined the impact of teacher cognitive and noncognitive abilities on student achievement. Using longitudinal data, the researchers studied the impact of middle school teachers' GPA in upper secondary school on student achievement. They found "that while high-ability students benefit from being matched to a high cognitive teacher, such a match is even detrimental for lower achieving students" (p. 26). They also found that low-performing students benefit from teachers with high social abilities, while teachers' social ability had negligible effect on high-aptitude students.

> *Low-performing students benefit from teachers with high social abilities, while teachers' social ability had negligible effect on high-aptitude students.*

These findings fly in the face of the growing call for recruiting top-scoring high school graduates into the teaching profession (Auguste, Kihn, & Miller, 2010; McKinsey & Company, 2007). Despite the lack of convincing evidence that teachers' academic performance in high school benefits all students (Gronqvist & Vlachos, 2008; Meroni, Vera-Toscano, & Costa, 2015; Rice, 2003), McKinsey, the globally influential consulting firm, has been urging nations to attract and retain the top-third high school graduates in careers in teaching (Auguste et al., 2010; McKinsey & Company, 2007). McKinsey's advice was based on its analysis of policies and practices in top-performing countries on PISA. The firm claims to have found that high-performing countries tend to recruit and retain top-scoring high school graduates in the teaching profession. For example, Singapore, Finland, and South Korea draw 100%

of their teachers from the top third of the academic pool, according to the authors of the McKinsey report. In contrast, only 23% of U.S. teachers come from the top third of college graduates—and in high-poverty schools, that rate drops to 14%. Hence, the authors believe that putting top scorers in classrooms will improve student achievement (Auguste et al., 2010).

McKinsey's suggestion amounts to another panacea solution in education. But apparently, as the Swedish study demonstrates, the McKinsey panacea, like all other cure-all education solutions, is no more than a myth, "an urban legend," as the Finnish education scholar Pasi Salhberg (2017) calls it. There is no evidence that Finland, a consistently high PISA performer, has been picking top academic performers to become teachers. Instead, the country that has received global admiration for its education has deliberately avoided using high school academic performance as a criterion for selecting teacher candidates because "the best students are not always the best teachers" (p. 60).

> *Teachers who were the best students can be the worst nightmares for low-achieving students.*

Worse yet, the teachers who were the best students can be the worst nightmares for low-achieving students, as the Swedish researchers found. The best students, when they become teachers, do not benefit their lowest-achieving students. On the contrary, they cause them harm. This is a perfect example of one of the major causes of adverse side effects in education: individual variability.

> *The effect of any treatment is the result of interaction between the characteristics of the treatment and characteristics of the individual.*

Just as people can have different responses to the same medical treatment because of individual variability in genes, environment, and life style, students can have different reactions to the same educational treatment because of their individual conditions. In other words, the effect of any treatment is the result of interaction between the characteristics of the treatment and characteristics of the individual. There is a long history of studying this interaction in education.

## APTITUDE-TREATMENT INTERACTION

In 1957, Lee Cronbach, one of the most prominent and influential educational psychologists in history, called on psychologists to study the "interaction of treatment and individual" in his essay "The Two Disciplines of Scientific Psychology," published in the *American Psychologist*. He observed the unhealthy and unproductive division in psychology between those who sought to develop an effective treatment that would apply to all individuals and those who focused on identifying unchangeable individual human traits. "Thus we come to have one psychology which accepts the institution, its treatment, and its criterion and finds men to fit the institution's needs. The other psychology takes man—generalized man—as given and challenges any institution which does not conform to the measure of this standard man" (Cronbach, 1957, p. 679).

While both lines of pursuit were meaningful, neither one was completely correct because "the persons treated usually are observed to differ in their response to treatment, and also to differ from one another in many other correlated ways" (Snow, 1991, p. 205). The questions regarding any treatment thus should go beyond the usual "what is best" or "how the treatment can be made better." An important additional question should be: Is the treatment best or better for whom, when, and why?, according to Richard Snow (1991), another prominent Stanford educational psychologist and close collaborator with Cronbach. "The aptitude–treatment interaction (or ATI) paradigm was invented to address these questions in consort," wrote Snow (1991) more than 3 decades after Cronbach's proposal in 1957:

*An important additional question should be: Is the treatment best or better for whom, when, and why?*

> ATI methodology is designed to take individual differences among treated persons into account systematically in treatment evaluation—to assess the degree to which alternative treatments have different effects as a function of person characteristics and thus determine whether particular treatments can be chosen or adapted to fit particular persons optimally. Beyond methods for assessing interactions among person and situation variables, however, the approach offers a framework for new theories of aptitude interpreted as personal readiness to profit from particular treatment situations. (p. 205)

Recognizing the interaction between treatment and individuals was a conceptual revolution in intervention sciences. It had great implications for education and other fields such as psychotherapy and medicine (Caspi & Bell, 2004; Snow, 1991). ATI quickly gained popularity among researchers who were interested in finding the best treatment for individuals instead of the

*Recognizing the interaction between treatment and individuals was a conceptual revolution in intervention sciences.*

average treatment. Educational researchers studied the effects of matching treatment with individual characteristics or aptitude. Instructional designers tried to design individualized learning programs according to the characteristics of individual students (Cronbach, 1975; Cronbach & Snow, 1981; Kieft, Rijlaarsdam, & van den Bergh, 2008; Snow, 1978, 1992).

Unfortunately, the problem of interactions between aptitudes and treatments is extremely complex. Due to this complexity and the failure of some researchers to follow the methodological advice of Snow and Cronbach, there was much inconsistency in empirical evidence of the existence of ATI (Cronbach, 1975; Snow, 1992). The inconsistent findings led many educational psychologists to ignore or reject the ATI phenomenon, calling it a fad (Corno et al., 2001). But it is no fad. "ATI are ubiquitous in education," wrote Snow in 1992 (p. 11), summarizing decades of ATI research.

ATI research has not resulted in significant practical improvements in education, or in clear identification of how aptitude interacts with treatment. (There are many reasons for this, but they are outside the scope of this book.) As result, interest in ATI has waned over the years. Today there is not nearly as much interest among educational researchers in ATI as before. However, ATI is extremely relevant today, as it was from the 1960s to the 1980s. Cronbach's and Snow's groundbreaking and visionary thinking and work provide an important foundation for future work on effects and side effects.

The most important contribution of ATI research is its empirical evidence of the ubiquitous existence of the phenomenon that individuals respond to the same treatment differently. Simply stated, the same treatment has different effects on different individuals. Individual characteristics play an important role in mediating the effect of treatment, a role that cannot be neglected. As Cronbach said in 1957: "If tranquilizers make everybody happy, why bother to diagnose patients to determine which treatments they should have? And if televised lessons can simplify things so that every freshman will enjoy and understand quantum mechanics, we will need neither college aptitude tests nor final examinations" (p. 678).

## LESSONS FROM ATI RESEARCH

There are other important contributions, of which the most relevant for understanding side effects are the continually refined conceptualizations of the complexity of interactions between treatment and individual, as well as the insightful definitions of aptitude and treatment.

## Interactions Are Complex

In the view of ATI champions, the interaction between treatment and characteristics of the individual is extremely complex. As researchers began reporting inconsistent findings, Cronbach (1975) realized that he had been "shortsighted not to apply the same argument to interaction effects themselves" (p. 119). In other words, the effect of a treatment is dependent not only on one of the characteristics of the individual but also on further variables. Essentially, interaction should not be limited to simply the first-order treatment with one characteristic.

This perspective on the complex and dynamic nature of interaction moves beyond simplistic views of the impact of educational interventions on individuals. The effect varies according to a host of interacting characteristics of individuals. The effect may be observed immediately, but also can be undetected until later. Thus, the effect, positive or negative, of a treatment must be examined in the context of multiple variables and over a long period of time.

## Aptitude Is More Than Intelligence

Cronbach and Snow also conceived aptitude to be much broader than its traditional definition. According to them, aptitude includes intelligence, abilities, personality, motivation, styles, attitudes, and beliefs. Moreover, aptitude is not conceived necessarily as a relatively stable trait. Instead, an aptitude is "a relational construct, interpreting the behavior of person-in-situation, and characteristics of the situation are as much a part of the definition of a particular aptitude construct as are characteristics of the person" (Snow, 1991, p. 206).

This conceptualization leads to an expanded set of individual characteristics that can mediate the effect of a treatment. Besides the traditional traits such as intelligence, personality, and motivation, the set can include race/ethnicity, immigration status, age, gender, social status, and physical attributes. More important, it can include familial variables such as parental education, income, and family structures. It also can include characteristics of the community one lives in. In short, the specific context and the general environment students are in can interact with the treatment, causing the same treatment to have positive effects, no effects, or adverse side effects on different students in different situations.

### Treatment Is Dynamic

Within the ATI framework, treatment also is defined broadly, "as any manipulable situation variable" (Snow, 1991, p. 206). This definition includes characteristics of the context and characteristics of the treatment. For example, whether an instructional method is implemented in small groups or large groups is a contextual characteristic of the treatment. When studying the effects of teachers' academic background on student achievement, the teachers' gender, age, religion, or even physical appearance is considered a characteristic of the treatment. "Although these variables are technically not manipulable, client experience is manipulable by assignment rules with respect to them," writes Snow (1991). "Just as aptitude is a relational concept, so too is treatment, because persons construct and adapt their situations to fit their own characteristics, at least to some degree" (p. 206).

## FROM EFFECTS TO SIDE EFFECTS

The purpose of the ATI paradigm is to look for the main effects of treatment. Its interest is to determine whether or to what extent a treatment is effective in causing the intended outcomes for individuals or groups of individuals with certain characteristics. The body of literature following the ATI paradigm contains evidence that the same treatment that produces positive main effects for people with certain aptitudes can lead to adverse unintended side effects for students with other aptitude patterns.

> The purpose of the ATI paradigm . . . is to determine whether or to what extent a treatment is effective in causing the intended outcomes for individuals or groups.

The findings of the Swedish study mentioned in the opening paragraph of this chapter, for example, suggest that high-GPA teachers have the intended main effect (raising academic achievement) for high-achieving students, but the effect is negative for low-achieving students (Gronqvist & Vlachos, 2008). This is similar to the adverse side effect of thalidomide for pregnant women. A similar observation was made in a study published in 1979 in the *American Educational Research Journal*: "Educated/secure teachers were quite unsuccessful with dependent and low achieving students who were in the control treatment. On the other hand, they did best with high achieving students in the control group" (Ebmeier & Good, 1979, p. 11).

There are more examples. Recall the debate about the effects and side effects of direct instruction discussed in Chapter 3. Here is more evidence that direct instruction affects different students in different ways, some positively and some negatively. A 1981 study by Janicki and Peterson found that the effectiveness of direct instruction was dependent on students' self-perception of personal control: Students who had a high internal locus of control did worse in math in direct instruction than in a small-group variation of direct instruction. The authors concluded that "direct instruction would be effective for external students,

> *Literature following the ATI paradigm contains evidence that the same treatment that produces positive main effects for people with certain aptitudes can lead to adverse unintended side effects for students with other aptitude patterns.*

who have a locus of control that matches the actual teaching situation, and detrimental for internal students, who may be frustrated in a situation where they have little control" (pp. 77–78).

There are ample examples in the ATI literature of potential negative side effects of the same interventions on students with different characteristics. Working memory capacity has been found to affect the effectiveness of different math instructional approaches (Fuchs et al., 2014). Students with low prior domain knowledge benefited from exploratory activities that preceded explicit instruction, but the same method had a negative effect on students with higher prior domain knowledge (Fyfe, Rittle-Johnson, & DeCaro, 2012). Dyslexic children's initial response variability when processing sounds was found have an impact on the degree to which they benefit-

> *Students with low prior domain knowledge benefited from exploratory activities that preceded explicit instruction, but the same method had a negative effect on students with higher prior domain knowledge.*

ed from wearing assistive listening devices to improve their phonological awareness and reading performance, with some benefiting more and others much less. And even worse, some experienced a negative effect (Hornickel, Zecker, Bradlow, & Kraus, 2012).

The body of ATI literature confirms one of the two most important mechanisms that cause adverse side effects in education: individual variability. It clearly shows that the same treatment can have different effects on students with different characteristics or aptitudes. For some students, the effect can be detrimental, certainly unintended by the developers of the treatment. In other words, one student's medicine can be another student's poison. Individual variability as a cause of adverse side effects is illustrated in the case of school choice programs.

## WHO GETS HURT: THE CASE OF SCHOOL VOUCHERS

School choice has been one of the greatest debates in American education for many decades, since the 1950s when the free-market economist Milton Friedman, a Nobel prize winner in economic science, proposed to turn public education into a free market (Carnoy, 2001; Fowler, 2002; Friedman, 1955; Greene, 2011; Willingham, 2017). The debate has become fiercer in recent years as many states have begun to implement various forms of school choice, such as public charter schools, magnet schools, and cross-district choices, resulting in greater levels of privatization and marketization (Ravitch, 2013). The election of Donald Trump as U.S. president in 2016 and his appointment of Betsy DeVos as Secretary of Education have made the debate even fiercer because of their strong support for school vouchers, that is, using public funds to support children attending private schools (Willingham, 2017).

> *The election of Donald Trump as U.S. president . . . and his appointment of Betsy DeVos . . . have made the debate even fiercer because of their strong support for school vouchers, . . . using public funds to support children attending private schools.*

The debate is centered on whether school choice ultimately improves American education. Proponents believe it does. Milton Friedman, sometimes called the grandfather of vouchers, and his wife Rose Friedman launched the Friedman Foundation for Educational Choice to "promote school choice as the most effective and equitable way to improve the quality of K–12 education in America" (Forster, 2016). Opponents disagree (Ravitch, 2013). There are many different points of contention, which include whether school choice negatively affects public schools and whether school choice results in social segregation. But foremost and most important is whether school choice leads to better achievement for students participating in the choice programs.

> *There are many different points of contention, which include whether school choice negatively affects public schools and whether school choice results in social segregation. But . . . most important is whether school choice leads to better achievement.*

Since the 1990s, empirical evidence has emerged. Both sides have been using the same body of evidence to argue for and against school choice, despite its imperfect nature. The central point of disagreement is the size of the effect. The same body of evidence has generated different conclusions (Carnoy, 2001; Forster, 2016; Lubienski, 2016; Shakeel, Anderson, & Wolf, 2016). Proponents seem to have found more significant positive effects of the programs than independent researchers (Carnoy, 2001).

> *Even if the programs did have positive effect on average, . . . we need to know whether or to what degree they caused damage to some students due to individual variability.*

But the debate has missed an important point. The debate has been concerned only about the effect on average, on everyone in the programs, resulting in efforts from both sides to argue over the size of either the positive effect or the negative effect. Lessons from ATI research teach us that we need to pay attention to individual variability. That is, the effect of school choice is dependent on individual characteristics. Thus, even if the programs did have positive effect on average, and this question continues to be debated, we need to know whether or to what degree they caused damage to some students due to individual variability.

### "The Win–Win Solution"

In May 2016, Greg Forster, a fellow at the Friedman Foundation for Educational Choice, released the 4th edition of a report about private school choice programs. As its title, *A Win-Win Solution: The Empirical Evidence on School Choice*, suggests, this series of reports aims to provide empirical evidence about the effects of school choice. Forster claims to have systematically reviewed publicly available empirical studies that used the "gold standard" of research methods—random assignment of participants. He concludes:

> The empirical evidence shows that choice improves academic outcomes for participants and public schools, saves taxpayer money, moves students into more integrated classrooms, and strengthens the shared civic values and practices essential to American democracy. (p. 1)

Essentially, Forster tries to advocate school choice as a panacea. He argues that empirical evidence obtained through the most rigorous research method shows that even the most controversial form of school choice, vouchers to send children to private schools, is a "win–win" solution for everyone in every aspect. Everybody benefits and nobody loses. Forster was not alone in relying on the gold standard of research design to buttress his argument for the effect of school vouchers. A group of voucher advocates at the University of Arkansas produced a report that shows positive effect

*Both reports have been criticized for their biased selection of studies and flawed analysis.*

of vouchers after "a meta-analytic and systematic review" of "the participant effects of private vouchers across the globe" (Shakeel et al., 2016, p. 1). Both reports have been criticized for their biased selection of studies and flawed analysis (Lubienski, 2016).

We are interested in side effects, adverse effects on groups of individuals with certain characteristics. There is no need to challenge Forster's selection of studies and analysis because his report and the studies present clear evidence of the existence of side effects due to individual variability.

## A Win–Lose Solution

Foster's claim about the academic benefits of choice for participants was based on 18 studies using random-assignment methods. He concluded that "this body of evidence shows that school choice benefits students":

> Fourteen studies find positive effects on school choice participants: six find choice had a positive effect across all students participating and another eight find choice had a positive effect on some student groups and no visible impact on other students. Two studies find no visible effect from choice. Two studies on Louisiana's voucher program find that it had a negative effect. (Forster, 2016, p. 10)

Forster's own data do not support his sweeping conclusion. Only six out of 18 studies, or about 30% of the studies, found positive effect across all students. The other eight studies Forster counted as having a positive effect actually had mixed results: positive for some and no visible effect on others. Furthermore, two studies found outright negative effect.

Judging from the evidence, school choice, just like all other educational interventions, is no panacea. It is subject to the law of aptitude–treatment interaction. Its effect is dependent on individual characteristics and contexts. The University of Arkansas report found that effect sizes of programs varied a great deal across countries and locations as well. The report's authors

*Forster's own data do not support his sweeping conclusion.*

found that the overall results "indicate that school vouchers have positive effects in both reading and math, but that these impacts are largest in programs outside of the US" (Shakeel et al., 2016, p. 33). Furthermore, they found no effect on reading in the United States but large positive effects in other countries, with the largest in Bogota, Colombia. This suggests that school choice programs can help or hurt depending on the context in which they are implemented.

## Effects of Contextual Variability

The contexts in which a treatment is implemented can mediate its effect and cause adverse side effects. In one context, the treatment may result in its intended main effect, while causing harm in another context. As illustrated by the evidence (Figure 6.1) Forster used, the voucher programs had different effects depending on location. The voucher program in Louisiana had negative effect, causing a decline in students' achievement (Abdulkadiroglu, Pathak, & Walters, 2015; Mills & Wolf, 2016). The voucher programs in Washington, DC; Charlotte; and Milwaukee all were found to have positive effect for all students, while the majority of the studies of the New York City program found the effect to be positive for some students, with no or negative effect on others, as did the program in Dayton. The one study of the Toledo voucher program found no visible effect.

There is not much research about what and how contextual factors interact with school choice programs, but there is no lack of speculation. In an attempt to defend school choice as a "win–win" solution, Forster explains the significant negative impact of the Louisiana voucher program, found by two studies (Abdulkadiroglu et al., 2015; Mills & Wolf, 2016), as the result of "poor program design and fear of future action from hostile regulators" that led to low participation of private schools (Forster, 2016, p. 12). Consequently, participating private schools "are likely to be the worst performing schools" (p. 13). Mark Dynarski (2016) argues that the negative effect may be due to the decline of quality of private schools and the narrowing gap in quality between public and private schools in Louisiana. The University of Arkansas report suggests that funding types can influence the effect of school choice programs. The report's authors found that publicly funded vouchers delivered larger effect sizes than privately funded ones, but the difference is largely influenced by the outsized effect of one publicly funded program in Bogota, Colombia.

*There are certainly . . . contextual variables, such as population density, transportation, culture, race/ethnicity mixture, and religion in a given location, that can influence the effect of school choice, resulting in positive, none, or negative impact on students.*

There are certainly other contextual variables, such as population density, transportation, culture, race/ethnicity mixture, and religion in a given

**Figure 6.1. Nature of Effect on Academic Outcomes of Choice Participants by Location***

| Location | Authors (Year) | Positive for All | Positive for Some | Negative | No |
|---|---|:---:|:---:|:---:|:---:|
| Louisiana | Mills & Wolf (2016) | | | X | |
| Louisiana | Abdulkadiroglu et al. (2015) | | | X | |
| New York | Chingos & Peterson (2015) | | X | | |
| New York | Bitler et al. (2015) | | X | | |
| New York | Chingos & Peterson (2013) | | X | | |
| New York | Jin et al. (2010) | | X | | |
| New York | Howell & Peterson (2006) | | X | | |
| New York | Krueger & Zhu (2004) | | | | X |
| New York | Barnard et al. (2003) | | X | | |
| New York | Howell & Peterson (2006) | | X | | |
| Washington, DC | Wolf et al. (2013) | X | | | |
| Washington, DC | Howell & Peterson (2006) | X | | | |
| Dayton | Howell & Peterson (2006) | | X | | |
| Charlotte | Cowen (2008) | X | | | |
| Charlotte | Green (2001) | X | | | |
| Milwaukee | Green et al. (1999) | X | | | |
| Milwaukee | Rouse (1998) | X | | | |
| Toledo | Bettinger & Slonim (2006) | | | | X |
| Total | | 6 | 8 | 2 | 2 |

*Adapted from Forster (2016). Some of the publication years in the original report are changed to match actual years of publication.

location, that can influence the effect of school choice, resulting in positive, none, or negative impact on students. Whatever the reason or combination of reasons, school choice is not a panacea. When it helps some, it is bound to hurt others. Thus, policymakers and parents cannot blindly adopt it or reject it without considering its effects and side effects.

## Effects of Student Variability—Tankers and Leapers

The effect of attending private schools supported by school choice varies a great deal among participating students and across cohorts. Some students benefited, but some were hurt. Also, there were "tankers"—students who fell more than 1.5 standard deviations—and "leapers"— students whose scores rose by more than 2 standard deviations. They greatly influence the overall effect of programs, suggesting the different effect on different students.

*The effect of attending private schools supported by school choice varies a great deal among participating students and across cohorts.*

Different sites also saw inconsistent patterns of effects across cohorts, with the Washington, DC, program the only site that showed relatively consistent achievement gains across grades (Carnoy, 2001).

What led to the tankers' decline and the leapers' improvement? Why was there so much inconsistency across cohorts? There is evidence that individual variability played a role. For example, a group of researchers from the University of California, Irvine, found that the New York City voucher experiment "did little to influence student achievement" but had "a small negative effect for a small group of high-performing students after the first two years of the program" (Domina & Penner, 2013, p. 24). Similar findings were reported by another group of researchers (Barnard, Frangakis, Hill, & Rubin, 2003). The NYC experiment also was found to have a negative effect on non-Black students in math achievement (Krueger & Zhu, 2004). The effect of the Charlotte experiment also found different effects on students with different characteristics. For example, the effect was large and negative for African American students with mothers who dropped out of high school, while the effect was positive for those with mothers who graduated from college and those living in a two-parent home (Cowen, 2008).

There may be adverse effects on students with other characteristics, but these studies do not systematically report them, perhaps because the researchers did not intentionally look for them in the data. It is also possible that the available data do not contain such evidence since interest has been on the overall effect instead of the effect on different individuals. It also should be kept in mind that the voucher programs have been designed to serve primarily low-income, minority students in urban areas. As a result, the student population studied is much more homogeneous than all students in American schools. Thus, when considering the expansion of school choice nationally, we must carefully study and report its effects and side effects on students with different sets of characteristics.

### Effects of Parent Variability

Even if school choice led to positive effect for all students, not all parents are willing or able to participate. Parental choice hence adds another variable that influences the effect of school choice as an educational treatment. Characteristics of parents have been found to affect their decision to accept vouchers and send their children to private schools.

*Characteristics of parents and the homes children live in can affect whether choice has positive, zero, or negative effect. . . . Evidence of the effect of voucher programs does not support Forster's rosy picture.*

John Witte, professor of political science and public affairs at the University of Wisconsin, studied the Milwaukee Parental Choice Program and wrote a seminal book on school choice based on his study. In the book, *The Market Approach to Education: Analysis of America's First Voucher Program*, Witte (2001) notes that African Americans and Hispanics are more likely than their White counterparts to apply to voucher programs like the one in Milwaukee, females are more likely to apply than males, and lower-income families are more likely to apply, as are mothers with higher levels of education. University of Chicago political science professor William Howell and Harvard University government professor Paul Peterson made both similar and different observations in their book, *The Education Gap: Vouchers and Urban Schools* (2006). In their studies, families with lower income were more likely to decline vouchers; there were more African American students among those who declined vouchers; and the mothers of students who declined had statistically significantly fewer years of education.

A more recent study of the voucher program in Charlotte found further evidence of the effect of parental characteristics. The researcher, Joshua Cowen, an education professor at the University of Wisconsin, found that parents who had attended some college were more likely to participate in the program. Students living in two-parent homes also were more likely to participate. African American parents were less likely to participate (Cowen, 2008). In summary, race, gender, education level, and family structure all mediate the effect of school choice on student achievement. Thus, characteristics of parents and the homes children live in can affect whether choice has positive, zero, or negative effect.

It is clear that the evidence of the effect of voucher programs does not support Forster's rosy picture that school choice is the cure-all treatment to the education problems in America. The effect is far from uniformly positive for all students. Instead, it varies a great deal depending on the characteristics of the context, the students, and their parents. The effect can be negative for some students.

## SUMMARY

One student's medicine is another one's poison. This chapter illustrates how negative side effects occur as a result of the interaction between students' characteristics and educational treatments. Whether they are education policies to recruit and retain top-scoring high school graduates to the teaching profession, funding private schools with public dollars or allowing parents to choose schools, or practices such as direct instruction approaches, they cannot possibly affect all students positively in a uniform fashion. We should always be mindful of the potential adverse effects on some students due to their individual characteristics.

> *Negative side effects occur as a result of the interaction between students' characteristics and educational treatments.*

By the way, all the studies on the effects of school voucher programs found the effects to vary across different subjects. Most of the studies reported effects on only two subjects: reading and math. Many of the studies reviewed by Forster found more positive effect on math achievement than on reading. For example, a study of the Milwaukee program found positive effect on math achievement of low-income, minority students, but the "effects on the reading scores are as often negative as positive and are nearly always statistically indistinguishable from zero" (Rouse, 1998, p. 584). This difference confirms another major mechanism of side effects discussed earlier: a broad range of desirable and potentially competing educational outcomes.

# CHAPTER 7

# The Futile Quest for Panacea

Wars, Pendulum Swings, and
Snake Oil in Education

"Mr. President, over the past decade, I have been continually puzzled by
our Nation's failure to produce better students despite public concern and
despite the billions of Federal dollars which annually are appropriated for
various programs intended to aid and improve education," stated Senator
Robert Byrd (D-WV) on the Senate floor during a debate about education
legislation (Byrd, 1997). After some remarks about the miserable standing
of American students' math achievement in comparison to other nations on
international assessments, presumably TIMSS, the senator called out the
culprit: "something called the 'new-new math.' Apparently the concept behind this new-new approach to mathematics is to get kids to enjoy mathematics and hope that that 'enjoyment' will lead to a better understanding of
basic math concepts. Nice thought, but nice thoughts do not always get the
job done" (Byrd, 1997).

Senator Byrd fired one of the numerous shots in the math wars in
California and across the country in the 1990s (Boaler, 2008; Klein, 2003,
2007; Schoenfeld, 2004; H.-H. Wu, 2000). He took aim at the reformers,
who promoted an integrated approach that made math instruction a jour-
ney of independent exploration because they were worried that students
could crunch numbers but couldn't use them thoughtfully, as a result of the
traditional "kill and drill" methods of math education.

"Whacko algebra," Senator Byrd called one of the algebra textbooks that
was aligned with the thinking and approach of the reformers. "Rainforest
algebra," "MTV algebra," and "fuzzy math" were some of the other phrases
used to show how ridiculous critics considered the reformers' pedagogy and
materials to be. Senator Byrd represented the "back-to-basics" camp, which
believed that math needs explicit instruction and that some things must be
practiced over and over until students develop automaticity. Thus, they accused the reformers of taking the math out of math education and blamed
them for the apparent decline in student math achievement.

It was called a war because the disputes between the two sides went way beyond disagreement between academic researchers and educators. It involved politicians like Senator Byrd. It involved parents, journalists, and the general public. It was fought in community centers and schools, in newspapers and on TV, and in Congress and state legislative bodies.

The war became so widespread and destructive that Richard Riley, Clinton's Secretary of Education, called for a cease-fire. "This [the math war] is a very disturbing trend," Riley (1998) told the attendees at the Joint Mathematics Meetings of the American Mathematical Society (AMS) and the Mathematical Association of America (MAA) on January 8, 1998. He added: "And it is very wrong for anyone addressing education to be attacking another in ways that are neither constructive nor productive" (p. 488). He forcefully argued for the "need to bring an end to the short-sighted, politicized, and harmful bickering over the teaching and learning of mathematics," because "if we continue down this road of infighting, we will only negate the gains we have already made, and the real losers will be the students of America" (p. 489). The war ended in the defeat of the reformers. Math education in California and elsewhere in the country went "back to basics."

## CYCLICAL WARFARE AND PENDULUM SWINGS IN EDUCATION

### The Math Wars

The math war in the 1990s was not the first math war. A similar war was fought some 30 years before, in the 1960s. In the wake of the former Soviet Union's successful launch of the first man-made satellite, Sputnik, America was in panic mode. Worried that the Soviet Union was surpassing the United States in science and technology, America enacted the National Defense Education Act (NDEA) in 1958. The law provided funds to support math, science, and engineering education in K–12 schools, among other things. Recognizing the inadequate achievement in math, the U.S. government funded projects to develop new math curricula and teaching methods. These projects resulted in the so-called new math (Knudson, 2015).

*The math war in the 1990s was not the first math war.*

The new math was a radical departure from traditional math. It emphasized inquiry-based learning and conceptual understanding over rote memorization and direct instruction. It quickly became popular in American classrooms. The traditionalists fought back, as exemplified by the 1973 book of New York University math professor Morris Kline, *Why Johnny Can't Add: The Failure of the New Math*. The new math movement practically ended by the mid-1970s, only to be resurrected in the 1990s, which, of course, caused another round of battles.

The math war continues today. The spirit of the new math did not go away. It continues to live today, in the Common Core math, according to University of Florida math professor Kevin Knudson (2015). Of course, not surprisingly, the Common Core math has not lacked critics among politicians, parents, educators, and researchers. Even the now-infamous comedian Louis C.K. joined the fight against the Common Core math (Mead, 2014).

> *The spirit of the new math did not go away. It continues to live today, in the Common Core math.*

The history of math education is in essence a history of cycles of wars. Every few decades, a war broke out and then settled with one side claiming victory and becoming the dominant approach in classrooms. But its dominance would erode as criticism and objections mounted. Then the opposite side would arise and became the new victor. The cycle would repeat itself some time later. As a result, math education has been "caught in a 200 plus–year pendulum swing between an overemphasis of rote practice of isolated skills and procedures and an overemphasis of conceptual understanding, with their respective overreliance on either teacher-directed or student-centered instruction," according to Matt Larson, president of the National Council of Teachers of Mathematics (NCTM), the organization that was partially responsible for seeding the 1990s math war (Larson, 2017).

> *Math education has been "caught in a 200 plus–year pendulum swing between an overemphasis of rote practice of isolated skills and procedures and an overemphasis of conceptual understanding."*

### The Reading Wars

The field of reading instruction has witnessed a parallel history of cyclical warfare (J. S. Kim, 2008; Pearson, 2004). "Controversy over the role of phonics in reading instruction has persisted for over 100 years, making the reading wars seem like an inevitable fact of American history," observed Harvard Graduate School of Education professor James Kim (2008, p. 89) in his thoughtful recounting of the reading wars. Horace Mann, for example, was a staunch critic of teaching phonics

> *The field of reading instruction has witnessed a parallel history of cyclical warfare.*

because he believed it would impede reading for meaning. Mann can be considered the early instigator of the whole-language camp in reading, which has been battling with the phonics camp in the multiple recurring reading wars over the past few decades.

In 1955, the phonics camp fired the first salvo at the whole-language camp, igniting the first major reading war. "The teaching of reading—all over the United States, in all the schools, and in all the textbooks—is totally wrong and flies in the face of all logic and common sense," declared Rudolf Franz Flesch in his book *Why Johnny Can't Read*, a book that would have a long-lasting impact on teaching reading in America in the following decades. The book took aim at the then-popular "look-say" approach of teaching reading, which taught children to recognize and say whole words. The look-say approach was the continuation of the tradition begun with Horace Mann. The approach was further developed by W. S. Gray in his influential book *On Their Own in Reading* (1960), first published in 1948.

Gray believed that word perception would help children develop independence in analyzing new words. Moreover, "he put word perception in its larger setting—understanding the flow of ideas in sentences, paragraphs, and longer passages; grasping implied meanings; responding to them; and fusing them with previous knowledge" (Strang, 1967, p. 116). Flesch attacked Gray's meaning-focused approach. He proposed that children should be taught "how letters represented sounds and how to blend those sounds to identify words" (J. S. Kim, 2008, p. 91).

*Why Johnny Can't Read* became popular. Flesch's message resonated with the public, which was concerned about the rise of the Soviet Union and decline of America. Citizens and politicians embraced his back-to-basics and phonics-first approach. The phonics camp won the reading war. As a result, phonics instruction became the dominant approach in reading instruction. But the victory did not guarantee its permanent dominance.

The whole-language camp did not go away. It made a spectacular comeback in the late 1980s. "Whole-language pedagogy formed the latest conventional wisdom in reading," observed James Kim (2008, p. 97). The rise of the whole-language pedagogy surprised P. David Pearson, who had been a professional educator for 25 years and had seen the coming and going of many fads and debates in education. Pearson, then an education professor and leading expert in reading at the University of Illinois, wrote in 1989:

[During the 25 years], never have I witnessed anything like the rapid spread of the whole-language movement. Pick your metaphor—an epidemic, wildfire, manna from heaven—whole language has spread so rapidly throughout North America that it is a fact of life in literacy curriculum and research. Furthermore, it is, like the phonics first movement in America, likely to remain a force that literacy researchers and curriculum developers will have to acknowledge for the foreseeable future. Unlike the open school movement of the early 1970s, it is not likely to die at an early age. (p. 231)

But again, as one might have expected, whole language was not going to dominate American classrooms for long. Phonics began to come back in the late 1990s and completely defeated the whole-language camp in the first decade of the 21st century. That is the story told in Chapter 2: The National Reading Panel's conclusions and the Reading First program made the phonics camp the victor again and backed it up with billions of government dollars. But since the failure of Reading First and NCLB, the direct instruction phonics approach has seen rising criticism. It would not be a surprise to see a full comeback of the whole-language camp in the near future.

**Change Without Being Different**

The history of the math and reading wars best exemplifies the pattern of changes in education: change without being different. Numerous changes, small and big, have been introduced into education over the years. These changes were introduced, often forced, by the winning side of different wars through government policies and financial investment. A large proportion of parents, educators, and researchers who had different views were not necessarily convinced of the merit of the changes. They resisted the changes and found ways to revise policies and programs. When their ideas became reflected in policies, they sought to replace the previous changes with changes of their own, prompting the pendulum to swing back.

*Education remains stuck in perpetual pendulum swings— lots of movement and action, but going nowhere.*

As a result, education remains stuck in perpetual pendulum swings—lots of movement and action, but going nowhere. It has been fighting the same war, despite all the changes. The battle lines remain essentially the same: explicit (direct) instruction versus inquiry-based learning, and phonics versus whole language. In spite of the mounting evidence gathered over the years, neither side has conceded. Despite the progress made in related fields such as psychology, neuroscience, and cognitive science, education continues to recycle century-old ideas.

*Despite the progress made in related fields such as psychology, neuroscience, and cognitive science, education continues to recycle century-old ideas.*

## THE ELUSIVE MIDDLE GROUND

"I am hopeful that we can have a 'cease-fire' in this war and instead harness the energies employed on these battles for a crusade for excellence in mathematics for every American student," pleaded Secretary Riley (1998, p. 488) at the aforementioned joint meeting of AMS and MAA. He believed that the way to end the math war was to look for the middle ground between the opposing sides. "I believe that there is a 'middle ground' between these two differing views of how to teach mathematics," said Riley (p. 489). Seeking the middle ground would bring an end to the "either-or" mentality that caused the war in the first place.

The middle-ground approach Secretary Riley advocated is perhaps the most commonly used strategy in attempts to end wars and settle disputes in education. The approach urges the warring factions to come together to find common ground so as to move forward. It is based on the assumption that both sides are right and wrong. Both have something offer. Good education needs to incorporate some strategies from both camps; hence, one of the most commonly used sentences in efforts to settle education debates is "both are needed." The approach also assumes that both are wrong in some respects, that neither one has the complete solution. The hope is to combine effective elements of the opposing approaches and create a "balanced" pedagogy.

One incarnation of the middle-ground approach is to seek consensus. Typically sponsored by independent organizations or government agencies, such as the NCTM, National Research Council, or U.S. Department of Education, groups of experts are asked to review the evidence and come up with recommendations that draw from the opposing sides. The hope is that the consensus will be accepted, if not enthusiastically embraced, by both sides. The National Reading Panel, for example, was claimed to be an effort to find consensus, based on scientific research, on effective ways to teach reading and thus end the reading wars. The National Mathematics Advisory Panel was established for the same purpose in the teaching of math.

However, the middle-ground approach has not worked. Riley's efforts did not end the math wars. In less than 2 years after his 1998 appeal for a truce in the math wars, he was accused of "reigniting the math wars" by conservative think tank Hoover Institute's Williamson M. "Bill" Evers, who later served as assistant secretary of education in the Bush administration and was selected to lead the "agency action team" at the Department of Education in the Trump-Pence transition in 2016. The math wars raged on. In 2004, a *New York Times* article reported on the math wars in New York under the title "The Class Multiplies, But the Math Divides" (Freedman,

2004). In 2015, a *Time* magazine reporter observed the return of the new math in an article with a *Star Wars*–inspired title—"The New Math Strikes Back" (Phillips, 2015).

The consensus-seeking efforts did not work well to end the wars, either. In 2006, the National Mathematics Advisory Panel was established by President Bush to find consensus and the middle ground in math education. The Panel released its final report in 2008. The report drew wide and swift criticism. For example, Stanford education professor Jo Boaler (2008) writes:

> The National Mathematics Advisory Panel's report presents a case of a government controlling not only the membership of a panel chosen to review research—a panel dominated by educational conservatives rather than mathematics researchers—but the forms of knowledge admissible in the public domain. In its adherence to government directions, resulting in the disregard of the field of mathematics education research, the Panel's report communicates the view that the government, rather than academic researchers, should decide on the forms of knowledge that are legitimate in our pursuit of understandings about ways to help children learn. When governments step in to control research and knowledge production, limiting the methods used by researchers and the forms of knowledge acceptable, to the extent that a whole field of research is invalidated, then it is time to acknowledge that America's celebrated freedom—of thought and inquiry—has been dealt a very serious blow. (p. 592)

The National Reading Panel did not settle the reading wars successfully, either, as discussed in Chapter 2. There has been no shortage of calls or serious attempts to end the wars, but the wars have not ended. Education continues to be caught in pendulum swings. The search for the middle ground, the balance, and the consensus has been elusive (Larson, 2017).

## THE QUEST FOR PANACEA

The elusiveness has a lot to do with the quixotic quest for panacea in education. Although reasonable people generally would not believe in the existence of such cure-alls, the misguided belief in universally effective policies and practices persists throughout the history of education. It remains prevalent today.

Policymakers are eager for solutions that work for all children, for all purposes, and under all circumstances so that they can develop policies that can be uniformly implemented in all schools. For example, the executive

order to establish the National Mathematics Advisory Panel in 2006 charges
the Panel to advise the U.S. President (and Secretary of Education) "on means
to implement effectively the policy to fos-
ter greater knowledge of and improved performance in mathematics among American
students" (National Mathematics Advisory
Panel, 2008, p. 71). President Bush wanted
the Panel to recommend "proven-effective and
evidence-based mathematics instruction" (p.
71). It was presumed that whatever the Panel
recommended would apply to all American
students. The National Reading Panel had the
same charge and made recommendations that
were expected to work effectively for all children.

*Although reasonable people generally would not believe in the existence of such cure-alls, the misguided belief in universally effective policies and practices persists throughout the history of education. It remains prevalent today.*

Education solution developers are equally eager to claim that they
have the solutions that work for all children under all circumstances.
For example, the National Institute for
Direct Instruction (2017) claims that Direct
Instruction works effectively for all students:
"Its creators, Siegfried Engelmann and Dr.
Wesley Becker, and their colleagues believe,
and have proved, that correctly applied DI
can improve academic performance as well as certain affective behaviors."
It further claims that DI has four main features "that ensure students learn
faster and more efficiently than any other program or technique available."
Similarly, the Success for All Foundation (2017) website says: "The results
continue to show how successful the Success for All approach to learning is.
Schools keep seeing dramatic jumps in student reading ability."

*Education solution developers are equally eager to claim that they have the solutions that work for all children.*

The quest for panacea solutions in education prevents education from
making meaningful progress in a number of ways, as explained below.

## Perpetuating Warfare and Pendulum Swings

In the quest for panacea, no middle ground is allowed. Education wars are
always settled in a "winner-takes-all" manner. When a particular solution
wins the favor of policymakers, it becomes the cure-all, prescribed for all
children, like the case of Reading First. Despite criticism and challenges, the
policies are to be implemented and educators are to be held accountable for
faithfully executing the solution in their practices.

Similarly, proponents of one solution rarely accept that there are better
solutions than the one they advocate. They are committed to their solution.

And they can always marshal more than enough evidence to show the effectiveness of their proposed solution. Negative evidence or evidence of no effect is cast away as professional or commercial jealousy, ideologically driven attacks, or poor implementation by practitioners. They refuse to concede that their solution may not work equally effectively in all contexts. As a result, they do not want to retreat to give room for a middle ground.

> Negative evidence or evidence of no effect is cast away as professional or commercial jealousy, ideologically driven attacks, or poor implementation by practitioners.

The pursuit of panacea precludes compromise and middle ground. It also powers pendulum swings by setting up for failure any solution claiming to be a panacea. Since no solution works equally well in all contexts, a given solution naturally works better for some students, some outcomes, and in some contexts, and may not work at all in others. Worse yet, it could have negative effects in other contexts.

Gradually, evidence of no effect and negative effect accumulates to erode initial confidence in the solution, as the story of Reading First exemplifies. At the same time, the critics, the other side that lost the previous war but has never truly given up completely, bring their solution back and show how their solution works better, especially in addressing outcomes that have been negatively affected. Together these two forces begin to affect the wind of politics and public opinion. Eventually, the old favorite becomes the loser and gives way to the new favorite, initiating another pendulum swing.

## Precluding Balance

The belief in and pursuit of panacea in education hamper practitioners' efforts to seek balance and find the middle ground. It has become popular to shift to teachers the burden of seeking the middle ground. Teachers are urged to break the pendulum swings and end the wars in their classrooms. "To move mathematics teaching and learning forward, we have to resist the urge to be pushed to extremes," writes NCTM President Matt Larson (2017). "We have to do our part to break the historic cycle of pendulum swings." But this sound advice is impractical due to the belief in panacea, for a number of reasons.

> Belief in and pursuit of panacea in education hamper practitioners' efforts to seek balance and find the middle ground.

First, teachers have experienced a panacea-driven education. Teachers tend to teach the way they were taught (Kennedy, 1991). The education they received has a significant impact on their own teaching practices. They are likely to have been "brainwashed" by the education they received, particularly preservice teacher education, which may be oriented to one view of education. E. D. Hirsch (2010) and other conservatives have charged that teacher education programs typically favor the child-centered approach. Thus, the panacea-driven educational environment is unlikely to help teachers develop the capacity to critically discern the advantages and disadvantages of instructional approaches.

> *Even if teachers are willing and able to seek the middle ground and flexibly apply what they believe is right for their students, they typically are not allowed to do so.*

Second, even if teachers are willing and able to seek the middle ground and flexibly apply what they believe is right for their students, they typically are not allowed to do so because they must follow the approach favored by policymakers, which is considered the panacea. After the phonics approach became the favorite instructional practice in NCLB, teachers were forced or taught to follow it faithfully.

Third, even without policy mandate, teachers are asked to implement an instructional approach with high fidelity when their schools adopt an education solution. The solution developers demand it. Almost all solution developers condition their success on faithful implementation, as exemplified by this statement of the National Institute for Direct Instruction (2017): "Correctly applied DI can improve academic performance as well as certain affective behaviors." If a teacher deviates, he or she is not applying DI correctly and thus would be ruining its effectiveness.

## Misguiding Policymakers, the Public, and Parents

The belief in panacea solutions also leads to widespread misinformation and misguides policymakers, parents, and the general public. When a solution is touted as a panacea, it cites only its best evidence to support its effectiveness. And the effectiveness is claimed to be universally applicable to all individuals or groups, as in the case of the Reading First program. But in reality, it may be effective only for a certain group of children for some

> *Belief in panacea solutions also leads to widespread misinformation and misguides policymakers, parents, and the general public.*

outcomes. As a result, policymakers, the general public, and parents are misinformed and misguided, convinced that the solution works for all. And when the reality becomes exposed, policymakers, parents, and the public realize that the solution has no effect or even a negative effect on some children.

No effect is in a way a negative effect because investment in the solution prevented policymakers and parents from seeking other solutions that might have helped the children. This is just like misdiagnosis of cancer. Although a cancer patient may have received harmless ineffective treatment, he or she may have missed the opportunity to be successfully treated, allowing the cancer to have deteriorated further.

## Defending the Past

The pursuit of panacea in education sometimes results in a tendency to defend the past. The belief in panacea can lead to the belief that what has been developed is already the best and there is no need for improvement. Thus, advocates devote effort to defending what they have instead of seeking betterment. Politically and financially, it is in the best interest of education solution developers to collect and report evidence of effectiveness instead of finding evidence of ineffectiveness, but finding evidence of ineffectiveness is motivation to refine the solution or seek to develop alternative solutions. It is also in the best interest of developers to selectively report evidence of effectiveness rather than admitting limitations of their solutions. But again, it is the recognition of limitations that motivates efforts to improve.

> The politically correct advice to find the middle ground or a balance between opposing views is scientifically irresponsible.

Moreover, while it may have a natural peace-making appeal, the politically correct advice to find the middle ground or a balance between opposing views is scientifically irresponsible. It essentially suggests that both sides have discovered effective educational approaches. Although both may have missed something, combining them would work well. But the reality is that one approach may work very well in some contexts, while the other does not work at all. Combining them actually would reduce the effectiveness of the former approach.

## NEGLECTING SIDE EFFECTS

The *Cambridge English Dictionary* defines *side effect* as "an unwanted or unexpected result or condition that comes with the desired effects of something." As discussed in previous chapters, progress in modern medicine owes much both to paying attention to effects and side effects as well as to the use of randomized controlled trials. Government regulations force developers to ensure that a medical product is both safe and effective before it can be approved for use. As a result, all pharmaceutical companies, willingly or unwillingly, must collect evidence of effectiveness and evidence of adverse effects. They must state clearly and prove with evidence what illness a product can cure. They cannot claim that it cures all ailments. They also must study and report the conditions under which a product is effective or likely to cause harm. It is this acute attention to both effects and side effects that has led to efforts to find ways to mitigate side effects or avoid them by inventing new medical products, thus leading to significant improvements.

But education is still stuck in the age of snake oil. Not only is the belief prevalent that there is a panacea solution to all problems for all people, but there also is a general refusal, on the part of advocates, to believe their solution would do harm. Few people, when they promote their interventions, seem to believe that educational interventions, whether policy, instructional method, or curriculum, can have adverse side effects. There are no government or professional regulations that require developers of educational interventions to study and report potential side effects. Virtually all research in education focuses exclusively on proving or disproving the effectiveness of an intervention. It is extremely rare to find a research paper that reports both the effectiveness and adverse effects of a product, teaching strategy, or policy in education. The What Works Clearinghouse (2014) does not make it a requirement to report side effects. Only the degree to which the intervention was effective is reported.

> *Virtually all research in education focuses exclusively on proving or disproving the effectiveness of an intervention. . . . The* What Works Clearinghouse *. . . does not make it a requirement to report side effects.*

The belief in panacea in education is one of the reasons that education does not have a tradition of investigating side effects. But it is not the only reason. The positive perception of education is another one. Education is universally perceived to be good, so that very few people automatically associate education with any adverse effects. Thus, when people consider educational interventions, they believe they need to know only whether the interventions are effective, without thinking about the possibility that they may do harm. Another possible reason is that damages caused by education may take a long time to be observed or felt, quite unlike negative reactions to medicine

> *Damages caused by education may take a long time to be observed or felt, quite unlike negative reactions to medicine.*

(although even in medicine, negative effects on health may appear only years later in some cases). It is thus rather difficult to study or find out about education's side effects.

It is also possible that the narrow definition of educational outcomes makes it hard to observe adverse effects. The prevalent definition of educational outcomes included in policies, educational studies, and school evaluations today is cognitive abilities in a few subjects, measured by standardized tests. Unsurprisingly, evidence of effectiveness in education has been measured almost exclusively with standardized test scores. There are other outcomes that are equally, if not more, important. Personal qualities, interest, creativity, critical thinking, self-regulation, motivation, psychological well-being, and engagement have all been proposed as important educational outcomes (Duckworth & Yeager, 2015; Partnership for 21st Century Skills, 2007; Wagner, 2008, 2012; Zhao, 2016a). Looking only at test scores provides us no knowledge about whether an intervention found to be effective in promoting cognitive abilities might adversely affect personal qualities and motivation.

## RAGING WARS AND NEW PANACEA: A SUMMARY

A total rejection of cure-alls such as the miraculous elixirs or snake oil popular in the 19th and early 20th centuries greatly contributed to the transformational changes in the field of medicine. By rejecting cure-alls, the medical field was able to seek cures for specific illnesses. The field also was able to consider the limitations of effectiveness for certain groups and people, and the emphasis on safety further led to the study of side effects, as discussed in Chapter 2.

For education to make similar progress, it needs to reject the quest for panacea and start to require the studying and reporting of side effects. Besides the reading and math wars, there are many other wars that have been ongoing. There is the century-old war between **child-centered education and curriculum-centered education**, which seeded the reading and math wars. The disputes over whether education should follow the child or prescribed content fuel wars in almost all aspects of education, from the pedagogy of all subject matter to curriculum, from school organization to the student–teacher relationship, and from teacher education to assessment. These wars cannot be settled

*A total rejection of cure-alls such as the miraculous elixirs or snake oil popular in the 19th and early 20th centuries greatly contributed to the transformational changes in the field of medicine.*

easily because fundamentally they are about outcomes of education, that is, what kind of products schools should produce: citizens for a democratic society, a workforce, or individuals to compete for social positions (Labaree, 1997). The purposes of education is an issue of value (Biesta, 2010), and empirical evidence does little to settle the dispute. But rejecting both sides of the dispute as a panacea and uncovering the adverse side effects of both can help policymakers, parents, and the public make informed decisions.

There is also the war over **charter schools, school choice, and privatization of public education** (Fuller & Elmore, 1996; Gorard, 1999; Ravitch, 2013). The evidence so far is extremely mixed and confusing, with abundant evidence supporting the effectiveness of charter schools and equally abundant evidence showing their ineffectiveness. Perhaps the war can be settled by abandoning the belief that school choice is a panacea, working for all children in all contexts and for certain educational purposes, but at the same time allowing the possibility that it can work in some contexts. Evidence of both effects and side effects also can help policymakers, parents, and the public to make informed decisions about policies and practices regarding privatization and school choice.

There is the war over **class size**, which is directly related to the war over **education investment** and spending (Hansen, 2013; Krueger, Hanushek, & Rice, 2002). There are many other ones, too: **grade retention, tracking, value-added teacher evaluation,** and **gifted and talented programs,** to name just a few. These wars and disputes can all benefit from ending the pursuit of panacea and studying and reporting side effects.

Education also has seen the introduction of new panacea solutions in recent years. These new panacea solutions have become popular, but are not without challenges. For example, as we have seen, instructional strategies promoted by **visible learning** (Hattie, 2008) have spread like wildfire in classrooms all over the world, but the work behind it has been called pseudoscience (Bergeron, 2017). **Growth mindset** (Dweck, 2006) and **grit** (Duckworth et al., 2007; Duckworth & Yeager, 2015) have caught the attention of education leaders globally as the new wonder drug to cure the ill of low academic achievement, but their effectiveness has been challenged (Credé, Tynan, & Harms, 2017). **Asian education** has risen to become the poster child of education success (Tucker, 2011, 2014), but it has been roundly criticized (Zhao, 2014).

The raging wars and continual emergence of panacea solutions in education are unlikely to stop if we do not take seriously the missed lesson from medicine and begin to study and consider in educational decisionmaking both effects and side effects.

# CHAPTER 8

# Study Side Effects Now

## A Call to Action

A child-centered curriculum recently was listed as one of the three "risk factors" that predict failure of new charter schools in a report published by the conservative think tank Thomas B. Fordham Institute (Nicotera & Stuit, 2017). The report is intended to guide the decisions of authorizers of charter schools. The other two risk factors are "lack of identified leadership" and "high risk, low dose," meaning "applications propose to serve at-risk pupils but plan to employ 'low dose' academic programs" (p. 5).

Although the report does not say it outright, the message to authorizers is simple: They should be very wary of "applications that propose to deploy child-centered, inquiry-based pedagogies, such as Montessori, Waldorf, Paideia, or experiential programs" (Nicotera & Stuit, 2017, p. 5), because "they are strong predictors of future school performance" (p. 11). Moreover, the three risk factors "are easy-to-spot and hard-to-game pieces of information found in the written content of applications" (p. 11).

The reason for listing "child-centered curriculum" as one of three risk factors is based on the finding that schools that follow a child-centered curriculum are less likely to produce the test scores that indicate educational quality. The report recognizes that child-centered pedagogies "are not intended to prepare students to shine on the kinds of assessments that are typically used by states and authorizers to judge school performance—in other words, the same tests that our research team used to judge quality for purposes of this analysis" (Nicotera & Stuit, 2017, pp. 5–6).

Interestingly, however, the report's authors acknowledge that "quality is in the eye of the beholder," because they found that "many of these child-centered schools aren't 'failing' in the eyes of their customers" (Nicotera & Stuit, 2017, p. 6). The report suggests that the parental satisfaction in child-centered schools may be misguided because, judging from the test scores, there is little evidence of student learning in these schools. "The parents who choose them may not care if they have low 'value added' on test scores" (p. 6).

"Schools exist not only to benefit their immediate clients but also to contribute to the public good: a well-educated society," assert the authors of the report (Nicotera & Stuit, 2017, p. 6). To make sure that all children are learning so as to build a well-educated society, the report suggests that charter school "authorizers must balance parental satisfaction with the public's right to assure that students learn" (p. 6).

Apparently, the authors of the Fordham report judge the quality of education according to test scores on assessments used by states and authorizers. But child-centered, inquiry-based instructional models "are not intended to prepare students to shine" on these kinds of assessments. Hence, they are deemed ineffective and a risk factor that charter school authorizers should consider when reviewing applications.

What's interesting is that the report says nothing about why parents seemed to be satisfied with the child-centered education. If parents do not care about low scores on standardized tests, what do they care about? It is hard to believe that any parent would not want a good education for their child. So the parents must care about something else. Furthermore, if the child-centered pedagogy is "not intended to prepare students to shine" on tests, what is it intended to prepare students to shine on? The report does not say.

> The division between progressive, child-centered, and inquiry-based education and academic curriculum-driven education is the power source that has fueled the reading wars, the math wars, the battles over direct instruction versus inquiry-based learning, the wars over standards and testing, and the wars over national curriculum.

The report exemplifies a century-old war between child-centered education and curriculum/content, and teacher-centered education. In the United States, that's the war between progressivism and academic traditionalism (Evers, 1998; Norris, 2004; Ravitch, 2001; Wraga, 2001). This war is the mother of all wars in education. The division between progressive, child-centered, and inquiry-based education and academic curriculum-driven education is the power source that has fueled the reading wars, the math wars, the battles over direct instruction versus inquiry-based learning, the wars over standards and testing, and the wars over national curriculum.

## WHY STUDY SIDE EFFECTS?

The war has been ongoing for a long time, with each side claiming its effectiveness in educating children and accusing the other of destroying children's future and, by association, the future of society. The war has stalled real progress in education. Both sides want to move forward but neither is willing to concede defeat. Centrists have urged both sides to find the middle ground, without much success, because both believe they have found the panacea for all education problems.

The only hope of moving forward is evidence. People seem to all agree that education should be a field that uses policies and practices based on evidence—not any evidence, but scientifically collected evidence. Randomized controlled trials, borrowed from medicine, have gained prominence as the gold standard for judging the quality of evidence in education. But the problem with RCT is that it says a lot about whether a treatment is effective for causing a certain result, but says nothing about whether the result is desirable, nor does it say anything about whether it causes other results. Thus, it does little to settle the dispute between progressive educators and academic traditionalists.

For example, the Fordham report about risk factors for charter schools shows evidence that a child-centered pedagogy results in lower scores, but parents do not care about scores, so they remain ardent consumers of the approach. Moreover, parents may want a school that is "not intended to prepare students to shine" on tests because they may believe that pedagogies to prepare students for tests cause undesirable results for their children.

> Parents may want a school that is "not intended to prepare students to shine" on tests because they may believe that pedagogies to prepare students for tests cause undesirable results for their children.

More evidence has been collected using RCT over the past 2 decades, but the war continues. Just collecting more evidence apparently has not worked and probably won't work in the future. What we need to do is collect valid and reliable evidence of all possible effects of a treatment, that is, evidence of all possible outcomes a treatment can cause.

## Making Informed Decisions

Collecting evidence of all effects of a treatment may still not settle the war because education is value-based (Biesta, 2010). Different people and different societies value different outcomes. For example, some people may value test scores in reading, but others may value a love for reading. Some societies want compliant citizens, while others may want more diverse and creative individuals. While a scientific approach to collecting evidence of all effects may not change people's values, it provides more information so that consumers can weigh the consequences of different alternatives.

For example, the East Asian education systems perhaps best represent the academic traditionalists' views of high-quality education, for their rigor, focus on core academic subjects, explicit teaching, and hardworking students and supportive parents. The East Asian education also has produced the evidence of effectiveness for academic achievement that matters to the traditionalists: consistently superior performance on international and comparative tests in math, reading, and science. This is why the traditionalists have held up East Asian education as a model for American education (Evers, 1998; Stevenson & Stigler, 1994, 2006; Tucker, 2011, 2014, 2016).

*Some people may value test scores in reading, but others may value a love for reading. Some societies want compliant citizens, while others may want more diverse and creative individuals.*

However, as many have observed and as was presented in Chapter 4 of this book, the East Asian educational treatments are equally effective in causing some other results. They have been found, for instance, to lead to a decline of confidence, less engagement with the subject, and a decrease of interest in the subject. Moreover, the systems are also effective in reducing talent diversity, stifling creativity, and discouraging independent thinking and inquiry. Furthermore, East Asian education has been found to result in excessive academic anxiety and pressure, poor physical health, less socioemotional competence, more suicidal students, and an overall negative sense of sociopsychological well-being (Jiang, 2010; Leung, 2002; OECD, 2017; Zhao, 2014).

These are the effects that have been observed in East Asian education systems. It is uncertain whether presenting both sets of effects would change the minds of die-hard believers on either side of the battle. But the information of good *and* bad, which is dependent on how one values education, certainly helps policymakers, school leaders, and parents to weigh the pros and cons so as to arrive at the best choice fitting their education beliefs.

For the same reason, that is, to make informed decisions, East Asian educators should be given more information about the other effects of progressive education. East Asia has admired American education for its effectiveness in producing a diversity of innovative and creative talents, happy and confident children, and socially adept and emotionally mature students. East Asian parents and students also are jealous of American children for their opportunities to participate in sports, music, and free plays; their relaxed school life; their equal status with teachers; their freedom from anxiety and pressure; and their interactions with society and nature. If at all possible, they don't want to care about test scores. This is why many East Asian parents, given the opportunity, pursue an American-style education either by coming to America or having their children attend an American-style school in Asia, and why East Asian countries have launched waves of education reforms to overhaul their education (Gao, 2003; J. Kim & Kim, 2014; K. H. Kim, 2005; West-Knights, 2017; Zhao, 2009, 2014, 2015a). The American education that East Asians admire may be a romanticized version, but it bears the hallmarks of progressive education.

Apparently, the East Asian admirers are not familiar with the criticism launched against progressive education's child-centered, inquiry-based pedagogies. They have not been informed that such pedagogies are a risk factor, a warning sign for poor-quality schools. They have not received the memos that accuse the progressive education movement at the turn of the century of causing the decline of math abilities in America. "Because this [progressive education] movement won, instead of raising the numeracy of the general public and ensuring it was better equipped to navigate the increasingly sophisticated technology and global economy, American schools allowed an entire generation of students to fall behind mathematically," charges a 2016 article in *The Atlantic* that called one of the most prominent progressive education advocates, William Heard Kilpatrick, "the man who tried to kill math in America" (Whitney, 2016).

E. D. Hirsch (2010), one of the most influential critics of child-centered education, shares the assessment of the outcomes of progressive education:

> By 1950, with new, watered-down schoolbooks and a new generation of teachers trained in specialized colleges for education, the anti-bookish, child-centered viewpoint had taken over the schools. The consequence was a steep decline in twelfth-grade academic achievement between 1962 and 1980, after which, despite vigorous reform efforts, reading and math scores on the federally sponsored National Assessment of Educational Progress have hardly changed.

Former U.S. assistant secretary of education in the Bush administration Williamson M. Evers, a fellow at the conservative think tank Hoover Institution, blames progressive education for America's poor standing in math achievement in comparison to Asian countries in his book *What's Gone Wrong in America's Classrooms* (1998). In fact, the entire collection of essays in this book, authored by prominent traditionalist scholars such as E. D. Hirsch, Reid Lyon, and Harold Stevenson, is about how progressive education gets it wrong and why the traditionalists are right.

However, due to the lack of a tradition of simultaneously investigating and reporting effects and side effects in education, the evidence of positive and negative effects often has been reported separately, frequently by parties that have significant conflicts of interests. The observers could be looking for evidence that supports their views and weighs against their opponents'

approaches. As a result, the credibility, validity, and reliability of the evidence are seriously compromised. We need independent
researchers to examine and report all the effects, main effects and adverse side effects, of
an educational intervention simultaneously.

> *We need independent researchers to examine and report all the effects, main effects and adverse side effects, of an educational intervention simultaneously.*

## Halting the Pendulum Swing

Having more complete information about the effects and side effects of educational approaches may not stop the ideological wars, but it can help halt
the perpetual pendulum swing, the recycling of old ideas. The education
pendulum is pulled toward one extreme when one side of the war wins political or public favor for its positive effects without consideration of its potential adverse effects. Gradually, when people become aware of its negative
side effects, or the unwanted and undesirable outcomes, they begin to look
for a new solution. At this time, an old approach that once was discarded
for its unwanted effects begins to look attractive and gradually pulls the
pendulum to the other extreme.

If information of both positive and negative effects of a policy, teaching
strategy, or instructional program is known, reported, and disseminated so
that people understand the pros and cons, it
is more likely that rational people will make
the effort to weigh the positive effects against
the negative effects before they make a decision. Such a rational and evidence-based decisionmaking process makes it less likely that
people will have unrealistic expectations of
only positive effects. They would know there
is no panacea. Moreover, they would expect
to deal with and possibly find ways to mitigate the possible side effects. And when negative side effects emerged, they would not be

> *If information of both positive and negative effects of a policy, teaching strategy, or instructional program is known, . . . it is more likely that rational people will make the effort to weigh the positive effects against the negative effects before they make a decision.*

surprised and think about abandoning the adopted intervention for a new
one. As a result, there would be fewer fads and recycling of ideas in education. Instead of completely replacing an idea with a new one, we should
work on improving it, which is an important lesson to learn from the emerging field of improvement science (Bryk, 2015).

The case of the early enthusiasm for NCLB is an example of lacking information about possible side effects that manifested later. It did not take long
for the limitations of NCLB to emerge, as discussed in Chapter 1. Gradually,

support for NCLB withered and the early enthusiasm turned into criticism and rejection by people in the field and the Obama administration. When the Obama administration was unsuccessful in replacing the law, it enabled states to receive waivers from NCLB requirements. Much of what the law promoted lost credibility, and even its primary goal of closing the achievement gap has been challenged (Hess, 2011; Zhao, 2016b). The same could happen to visible learning. Given the Holy Grail label attached to it and its rapid spread across the world without consideration of its potential adverse side effects, the enthusiasm would be expected to wane eventually.

### Stimulating Innovation

The lack of concern for side effects perpetuates panacea thinking, which often stops innovation. Educational intervention developers are caught in the pursuit of cure-all programs and policies, expecting their solutions will have only positive effects. Few developers voluntarily examine the potential side effects of their interventions, because the side effects, if discovered and reported, could pose a threat to a developer's commercial or academic interests. If the intervention is believed to be effective for all people and all outcomes, there is naturally no room for improvement. What's left is only to defend the intervention's effectiveness when side effects are uncovered. Such is the case with Direct Instruction, whose proponents have cast evidence of its side effects as myths, as discussed in Chapter 3.

Admitting that no educational treatment can be universally effective helps redirect the efforts wasted on ideological quarreling to improving the treatment's effectiveness and minimizing negative side effects. Minimizing negative effects is itself advancement and should benefit the developers of treatments. The case of the $6 billion Reading First program, which advocated explicit teaching or direct instruction, is illustrative. The program was promoted as the cure-all for America's reading problems. Then-U.S. Secretary of Education Margaret Spellings likened it to the cure for cancer be-

> *If side effects had been considered, the Reading First Program probably would have been conceived and implemented differently.*

cause it was rooted in scientific research and fact. However, the "scientific research and fact" did not study side effects. So there was no information about its effectiveness for all students and all educational outcomes, not even outcomes in all aspects of reading abilities. As discussed in Chapter 2, the final evaluation found that the program did not significantly improve reading comprehension and thus deemed it a failure. However, the reality may be that the program had a positive effect for some students, no impact for others, and a negative effect on still others (Gamse, Jacob, et al., 2008).

If side effects had been considered, the Reading First Program probably would have been conceived and implemented differently. More important, if proponents of direct instruction were willing to investigate possible adverse effects, they would have more information about how the effects vary across different populations of students, due to ATI, and across different outcomes. As a result, they could have worked to develop a more effective treatment for some students and avoided applying the Reading First program to some others. The program then would not have been deemed a complete failure. Instead, we would have built on it and continued to improve it, if we had information on how it affected different outcomes for different students. Now all we have is another round of battles, with proponents wasting time defending its effectiveness and opponents criticizing it.

## Avoiding Education Malpractice

Studying and reporting side effects can help avoid education malpractice, which can hurt students, by providing guidance for better implementation of interventions. In medicine, consumers are always informed of effects and side effects so they can make informed decisions. Furthermore, information is provided about conditions under which negative side effects can occur for a particular population. For instance, specific warnings are given relating to certain populations, for example, children under a certain age, pregnant women, and people with certain preexisting conditions. Medicine that can cause adverse side effects when taken with other medicine or mixed with alcohol also has warning information for its intended consumers.

But educational interventions have always been sold to schools, parents, and students without warnings about side effects. Little is known about the specific conditions under which particular interventions will have their intended effect on student outcomes or the potential side effects of adopting those interventions. Thus, when adopted, interventions likely will have variable effects, including promoting the desired educational outcomes in some students, but not others; and promoting some outcomes at the cost of other equally (or even more) desirable outcomes. Having information about side effects, particularly the conditions under which negative side effects occur, can help guide proper implementation of educational interventions and avoid inadvertent malpractice.

## WHY HAVEN'T WE?

What works can hurt. Educational programs, approaches, and policies are indeed not unlike medical products: When they cure, they can hurt. There is emerging evidence pointing to the existence of negative side effects of educational approaches, programs, and policies, although the evidence has often been collected by critics with the intention of disproving the effectiveness of a particular intervention, rather than by the intervention's developers and advocates voluntarily. This suggests that negative side effects not only exist but also have not gone entirely unnoticed.

The literature suggests that side effects in education occur for primarily two reasons. First, the variability of conditions of individual students interacts with the treatment, making it impossible to have one treatment that causes positive effects for all students, as ATI theory and research have demonstrated. As a result, the effects can vary from positive to none to negative depending on the individual characteristics of students. In other words, the same treatment can help some students and hurt others. Second, the varying nature of the broad spectrum of educational outcomes makes it impossible for one treatment to have a uniform effect on all educational outcomes. Consequently, the effects of a treatment can boost one outcome, but hinder others.

Treating side effects in education the same way as in medicine can help resolve artificially divisive issues in education and advance the field. However, the negative effects of educational products have not been treated the same way as side effects of medical products, in a number of crucial ways.

First, there is no regulation that asks developers of educational treatments to examine and disclose potential side effects when providing evidence for their effectiveness. As a result, the majority of educational product and policy developers and proponents have focused exclusively on marshaling evidence to show their benefits and positive effects. Even review and synthesis studies, such as the numerous meta-analysis studies, have been devoted to proving or disproving the effectiveness of certain approaches or policies (e.g., Hattie, 2008; Shakeel et al., 2016; What Works Clearinghouse, 2014), without attention to potential negative effects. Thus, consumers (teachers, parents, education leaders, students, and the public) have information only about what works, without knowledge of the potential associated costs. In cases where potential damages may be greater than

> *Treating side effects in education the same way as in medicine can help resolve artificially divisive issues in education and advance the field.*

benefits, it perhaps would be better not to adopt the product even if it is effective in some way.

Second, the negative effects of educational products, when occasionally discovered, are not considered an inherent quality of the product or policy. Rather, they often are treated as unintended or unanticipated consequences or results of poor implementation. While not all negative effects can be anticipated and it is reasonable to believe that policymakers or product developers in education intend to do no harm, some negative effects can be predicted, based on past experience and sound reasoning, in advance of their actualization. For example, the side effects or collateral damages of NCLB could have been anticipated based on Campbell's law, which states: "The more any quantitative social indicator is used for social decision-making, the more subject it will be to corruption pressures and the more apt it will be to distort and corrupt the social processes it is intended to monitor" (Campbell, 1976, p. 49). The corruption cases reported by Nichols and Berliner in their 2007 book resulted from NCLB and could have been avoided or at least mitigated had the policymakers heeded the warning of Donald Campbell.

Third, when side effects in education occasionally are reported, they often come from opponents and critics of the products. But the opponents and critics often do not consider impartially the effects of the product or policy, nor do they have access to or resources to conduct original studies concerning it. As a result, the reported side effects often are brushed aside as lacking objectivity or scientific rigor, or as motivated by ideology. This is one of the reasons behind the long-lasting "wars" in education—two bodies of opposing literature that coexist in parallel places without much genuine interaction. As a result, much energy is wasted in research that does not lead to improvement.

Education as a field has been slow to improve because it largely has failed to build on past experience (Bryk, 2015). One way to build on past experience is to consider side effects as an integral aspect of research. Research on side effects can incentivize product and policy developers to improve their products and policies so as to minimize side effects or to develop alternative products and policies that cause less damage. It also can better guide consumers in choosing the products and policies that best suit them, considering both effects and side effects. Moreover, seeking to understand side effects can prevent damaging products and policies, despite their effectiveness, from being adopted. If the risks of a product are greater than its benefits, it should not be allowed to enter schools.

> *Education as a field has been slow to improve.*

## A CALL TO ACTION

This book is intended to build a strong case for treating effects of educational treatments the same way as the medical field treats effects of medical products: effects and side effects as two sides of the same coin. Assuming it has successfully convinced readers that the case is solid, we need to take actions to transform education into a field that pays equal attention to effects

*We need to take actions to transform education into a field that pays equal attention to effects and side effects.*

and side effects. This transformation is not easy but can be done, as the history of medicine shows. Merely about 100 years ago, the medical field "was a menacing marketplace filled with products such as William Radam's Microbe Killer and Benjamin Bye's Soothing Balmy Oils to cure cancer," according to John Swann, a historian at the Food and Drug Administration, as cited by Michelle Meadows (2006) in her reflection of the history of the FDA. "Products like these were, at minimum, useless remedies that picked the pocket of the user, but they could also be downright harmful." A hundred years later, we have a completely transformed medical field.

The transformation of medicine happened because of the collective, not necessarily coordinated, efforts of the public, scientists, government agencies, and the media. The transformation of education will need similar collective efforts. Everyone has a role to play.

### The Public and Consumers

The public and consumers played a significant role in the transformation of medicine. The women's clubs and the National Consumers League were instrumental in the enactment and enforcement of America's first food and drug law, the Pure Food and Drug Act of 1906, also known as the Wiley Act, named after Dr. Harvey Wiley for his significant work leading to the passage of the law. "Historians and Dr. Wiley himself credit the club women of the country for turning the tide of public opinion in favor of the 'pure food' bill," wrote FDA historian Wallace Janssen (1981).

To transform education, the public and consumers can play an equally significant role. Consumers of educational research, policy, and products should keep in mind that there is no panacea in education and thus should be concerned about potential negative effects of educational policies, programs, and instructional approaches. They should ask for information about both effects and side effects of educational interventions. For example, when publishers come to promote their products, school leaders, teachers, and parents should always ask for information about side effects of the products. Moreover, the public can take a more active role in demanding that the government, from federal to local agencies, such as school boards, require information about the potential side effects of new interventions to be introduced to their schools.

## Governments

The establishment of the FDA and the enactment of various laws regulating the drug industry were pivotal for the transformation of medicine. While it may not be realistic in the short term to expect the federal government to take similar actions in the field of education, governments at various levels can take immediate action. For example, the federal clearinghouse for educational treatments, What Works Clearinghouse, should consider and include in its reviews information about the negative effects of educational approaches, methods, products, or policies. This action would serve two purposes. First, it would serve as encouragement for educational researchers and product developers to seriously consider side effects. Second, it would provide consumers—educators, parents, and policymakers—with information for making informed decisions.

Federal research funding agencies such as the U.S. Department of Education—in particular, the National Institute of Education Sciences—and the National Science Foundation can consider in their funding decisions whether studies propose examining and reporting side effects. For example, they could start by including the investigation of side effects as a priority criterion to encourage research studies that explore both effects and side effects. When the time comes, they could require all studies that aim to develop new educational treatments to examine and report both effects and side effects.

Furthermore, federal agencies should devote funds to research programs that build theories, uncover new constructs and develop new measures, improve research designs and methodologies, and advance statistical modeling for studying both effects and side effects. This is of particular importance for transforming education because, despite the emerging evidence of side effects, there is no clear theorization or empirical verification of different relationships between different outcomes for different populations. It is also likely that investigating effects and side effects in the same study would require new methodologies and statistical modeling. Moreover, there may be important constructs of educational outcomes that have not been discovered. Finally, many proposed educational outcomes need better measurement instruments, and these need to be developed.

Governments at the state and district level can take some actions, too. The United States is fortunate to have a decentralized education system that allows local actions without federal mandates. States can independently enact and enforce regulations that require vendors of educational products to disclose information about potential side effects before the products are allowed to be marketed in their schools. Local school boards can take similar actions.

## Educational Researchers

Scientists played a vital role in the medical transformation not only with scientific discoveries but also with their actions to educate the public about the dangers of drugs. Before the FDA was established, medical doctors took action in screening and publishing findings of negative side effects of drugs. Educational researchers, as social scientists, have a similarly vital role to play in transforming education.

First, educational researchers should always be mindful that negative side effects occur and should voluntarily investigate and report side effects in their research. Those engaged in developing new educational treatments, such as programs and instructional strategies, should be particularly conscious of the "do no harm" advice in the medical field and actively examine and report possible adverse side effects. Those engaged in program evaluation should avoid looking for evidence of the existence of only positive effects. They should examine what damages a program might have done. For example, when looking at school privatization and vouchers, we cannot claim success because participants' test scores are better (Shakeel et al., 2016). We also must look at the potential negative impacts on the development of participants' other abilities, on teachers, and even on nonparticipating students affected by the program.

*The educational research community should consider studying and reporting side effects as an ethical issue.*

Second, the educational research community should consider studying and reporting side effects as an ethical issue. The Code of Ethics of the American Educational Research Association (AERA, 2011), the primary professional organization of educational researchers, already includes the "avoiding harm" statement: "Education researchers take reasonable steps to avoid harm to others in the conduct of their professional work. When unanticipated negative consequences occur, education researchers take immediate steps to minimize harm, including, if necessary, terminating the work." But this view of avoiding harm is reactionary because the actions are to be taken after negative consequences occur. We need to be more proactive. Thus, a revision of the statement could be something like: "Education research workers actively and voluntarily anticipate and investigate negative consequences . . . "

Third, leading research organizations such as AERA and academic journals can require research articles to include both main effects and side effects. Such a requirement would force or encourage educational researchers to pay attention to side effects in their studies. It is not likely that a government organization like the FDA would issue such a requirement, but it is quite possible for leading organizations and journals to start the movement.

Fourth, the research community should take seriously reports of side effects after the implementation of interventions. Instead of discarding such reports as unfair or biased criticism, uninformed myths, unintended consequences, improper implementation, or simply complaints by unhappy parents, students, or teachers, researchers and developers of educational interventions should bear the responsibility to investigate and respond to such reports. The FDA monitors side effects and recalls products all the time when a product's risks outweigh its benefits.

### The Media and Social Media

The media has been crucial in the transformation of medicine. In the campaign to pass the first food and drug law in America, for example, "national magazines such as *Collier's Weekly*, the *Ladies Home Journal*, and *Good Housekeeping*, aroused public opinion with their cartoons, articles, and editorials," writes FDA historian Wallace Janssen (1981). "A single chapter in Upton Sinclair's novel, *The Jungle*, precipitated legislation expanding federal meat regulation to provide continuous inspection of all red meats for interstate distribution, a far more rigorous type of control than that provided by the pure food bill."

The media and social media today can make a significant contribution to education improvement by advocating for the study of side effects and discussing both effects and side effects in their coverage, instead of just focusing on one or the other. Although eliminating important contributing causes from the initial diagnosis may have guaranteed its failure, if the coverage of No Child Left Behind had included effects and side effects together in the same piece of reporting more often, we might be in a different place in education.

## SIDE EFFECTS OF STUDYING SIDE EFFECTS: CONCLUSION

No doubt these recommended actions also have side effects that need to be addressed. One of the anticipated side effects of studying and reporting side effects along with intended main effects is increased regulations and requirements for educational product developers and researchers from governments, funding agencies, professional organizations, and academic journals and conferences. Another one would be the extra resources needed to investigate side effects in educational studies, which may result in added burdens on some developers and researchers. Another possible side effect of studying side effects would be too much information about an intervention, which could lead to confusion, indetermination, and delay of implementation.

But when we begin to address the side effects of these recommendations, education will have advanced. This is how we improve.

# References

Abdulkadiroglu, A., Pathak, P. A., & Walters, C. R. (2015). *School vouchers and student achievement: First-year evidence from the Louisiana Scholarship Program*. Cambridge, MA: National Bureau of Economic Research.

Abramson, L. (2007, July 27). Funds for "Reading First" program in peril. *National Public Radio*. Retrieved from www.npr.org/templates/story/story.php?storyId=12295349

Adams, G. L., & Engelmann, S. (1996). *Research on direct instruction: 25 years beyond DISTAR*. Seattle, WA: Educational Achievement Systems.

American Educational Research Association (AERA). (2011, February). Code of ethics: American Educational Research Association. Retrieved from www.aera.net/Portals/38/docs/About_AERA/CodeOfEthics(1).pdf

Anderson, L. W., & Sosniak, L. A. (1994). *Bloom's taxonomy*. Chicago, IL: University of Chicago Press.

Anderson, L. W., Krathwohl, D. R., Airasian, P., Cruikshank, K., Mayer, R., Pintrich, P., . . . Wittrock, M. (2001). *A taxonomy for learning, teaching and assessing: A revision of Bloom's taxonomy*. New York, NY: Longman.

The Annie E. Casey Foundation. (2010). *Early warning! Why reading by the end of third grade matters*. Retrieved from www.aecf.org/m/resourcedoc/AECF-Early_Warning_Full_Report-2010.pdf

The Annie E. Casey Foundation. (2013). *Early warning confirmed: A research update on third-grade reading*. Retrieved from www.aecf.org/m/resourcedoc/AECF-EarlyWarningConfirmed-2013.pdf

Arrow, K., Bowles, S., & Durlauf, S. (Eds.). (2000). *Meritocracy and economic inequality*. Princeton, NJ: Princeton University Press.

The Aspen Institute (Producer). (2012, September 29). Reversing the middle-class jobs deficit [Panel discussion]. Retrieved from www.aspenideas.org/session/reversing-middle-class-jobs-deficit-0

Auguste, B. G., Kihn, P., & Miller, M. (2010). *Closing the talent gap: Attracting and retaining top-third graduates to careers in teaching: An international and market research-based perspective*. New York, NY: McKinsey.

Bailey, M. J., & Dynaski, S. M. (2011). Inequality in postsecondary education. In G. J. Duncan & R. J. Murnane (Eds.), *Whither opportunuty? Rising inequality, schools, and children's life chances* (pp. 117–132). New York, NY/Chicago, IL: Russell Sage Foundation/Spencer Foundation.

Bailey, N. E. (2013). *Misguided education reform: Debating the impact on students.* Lanham, MD: Rowman & Littlefield Education.

Baker, K. (2007). Are international tests worth anything? *Phi Delta Kappan, 89*(2), 101–104.

Ballentine, C. (1981). Taste of raspberries, taste of death: The 1937 elixir sulfanilamide incident. Retrieved from www.fda.gov/AboutFDA/WhatWeDo/History /ProductRegulation/ucm2007257.htm

Barber, M., Donnelly, K., & Rizvi, S. (2012). *Oceans of innovation: The Atlantic, the Pacific, global leadership and the future of education.* Retrieved from www .ippr.org/publications/oceans-of-innovation-the-atlantic-the-pacific-global -leadership-and-the-future-of-education

Barnard, J., Frangakis, C. E., Hill, J. L., & Rubin, D. B. (2003). Principal stratification approach to broken randomized experiments: A case study of school choice vouchers in New York City. *Journal of the American Statistical Association, 98*(462), 299–323.

BBC. (Producer). (2011). Steve Wozniak: "Think for yourself." Retrieved from news.bbc.co.uk/today/hi/today/newsid_9661000/9661755.stm

Becker, W. (1977). Teaching reading and language to the disadvantaged—What we have learned from field research. *Harvard Educational Review, 47*(4), 518–543.

Becker, W. C., & Gersten, R. (1982). A follow-up of Follow Through: The later effects of the direct instruction model on children in fifth and sixth grades. *American Educational Research Journal, 19*(1), 75–92.

Beghetto, R. A. (2013). *Killing ideas softly? The promise and perils of creativity in the classroom.* Charlotte, NC: Information Age.

Beghetto, R. A. (2017). Legacy projects: Helping young people respond productively to the challenges of a changing world. *Roeper Review, 39*(3), 1–4.

Beghetto, R. A., & Kaufman, J. C. (2010). *Nurturing creativity in the classroom.* New York, NY: Cambridge University Press.

Bereiter, C. (1986). Does direct instruction cause delinquency? *Early Childhood Research Quarterly, 1*(3), 289–292.

Bereiter, C., & Kurland, M. (1981). A constructive look at Follow Through results. *Interchange, 12*(1), 1–22.

Bergeron, P.-J. (2017). How to engage in pseudoscience with real data: A criticism of John Hattie's arguments in visible learning from the perspective of a statistician. *McGill Journal of Education/Revue des Sciences de l'Éducation de McGill, 52*(1), 237–246.

Berliner, D. C. (2006). Our impoverished view of educational reform. *Teachers College Record, 108*(6), 949–995.

Bettinger, E., & Slonim, R. (2006). Using experimental economics to measure the effects of a natural educational experiment on altruism. *Journal of Public Economics, 90*(8-9), 1625–1648.

Bidwell, A. (2015, March 16). Racial gaps in high school graduation rates are closing. *USA Today.* Retrieved from www.usnews.com/news/blogs/data-mine/2015/03/16 /federal-data-show-racial-gap-in-high-school-graduation-rates-is-closing

Bieber, T., & Martens, K. (2011). The OECD PISA study as a soft power in education? Lessons from Switzerland and the US. *European Journal of Education, 46*(1), 101–116. doi:10.1111/j.1465-3435.2010.01462.x

Biesta, G. J. (2010). Why "what works" still won't work: From evidence-based education to value-based education. *Studies in Philosophy and Education, 29*(5), 491–503.

Bitler, M., Domina, T., Penner, E., & Hoynes, H. (2015). Distributional analysis in educational evaluation: A case study from the New York City voucher program. *Journal of Research on Educational Effectiveness, 8*(3), 419–450.

Bloom, B., Englehart, M., Furst, E., Hill, W., & Krathwohl, D. R. (1956). *Taxonomy of educational objectives: The classification of educational goals. Handbook I: Cognitive domain.* New York, NY: Longmans.

Boaler, J. (2008). When politics took the place of inquiry: A response to the National Mathematics Advisory Panel's review of instructional practices. *Educational Researcher, 37*(9), 588–594.

Bonawitza, E., Shaftob, P., Gweonc, H., Goodmand, N. D., Spelkee, E., & Schulzc, L. (2011). The double-edged sword of pedagogy: Instruction limits spontaneous exploration and discovery. *Cognition, 120*(3), 322–330.

Boylan, M. (2016, December 11). Here's why East Asian students consistently outpace their Western peers. *Business Insider.* Retrieved from www.businessinsider.com/heres-why-east-asian-students-consistently-outpace-their-western-peers-2016-12

Bray, M., & Lykins, C. (2012). *Shadow education private supplementary tutoring and its implications for policy makers in Asia.* Retrieved from www.adb.org/publications/shadow-education-private-supplementary-tutoring-and-its-implications-policy-makers-asia

Brent, G., & DiObilda, N. (1993). Effects of curriculum alignment versus direct instruction on urban children. *The Journal of Educational Research, 86*(6), 333–338.

Brown, N. (2013, August 5). Book review: *Visible learning.* Retrieved from academiccomputing.wordpress.com/2013/08/05/book-review-visible-learning/

Brunello, G., & Schlotter, M. (2010). *The effect of noncognitive skills and personality traits on labour market outcomes.* Retrieved from ftp.iza.org/dp5743.pdf

Bryk, A. S. (2015). *Learning to improve: How America's schools can get better at getting better.* Cambridge, MA: Harvard Education Press.

Buchsbauma, D., Gopnika, A., Griffiths, T. L., & Shaftob, P. (2011). Children's imitation of causal action sequences is influenced by statistical and pedagogical evidence. *Cognition, 120*(3), 331–340.

Bush, G. W. (2002, January 8). President signs landmark No Child Left Behind education bill. Retrieved from georgewbush-whitehouse.archives.gov/news/releases/2002/01/20020108-1.html

Byrd, R. (1997). A failure to produce better students. *Congressional Record, 143*(79), S5393. Retrieved from www.stolaf.edu/other/extend/Expectations/byrd.html

Campbell, D. T. (1976). *Assessing the impact of planned social change.* Retrieved from www.sciencedirect.com/science/article/pii/014971897990048X

Carey, T. (2015, January 16). China's educational success is taking a toll on students. *New Republic*. Retrieved from newrepublic.com/article/120794/chinese -education-system-prizes-intense-hard-work

Carnine, D. (2000). *Why education experts resist effective practices (and what it would take to make education more like medicine)*. Washington, DC: Thomas B. Fordham Foundation.

Carnine, D. W., Silbert, J., Kame'enui, E. J., & Tarver, S. G. (2004). *Direct instruction reading*. New York, NY: Prentice Hall.

Carnoy, M. (2001). *School vouchers: Examining the evidence*. Washington, DC: Economic Policy Institute.

Caspi, O., & Bell, I. R. (2004). One size does not fit all: Aptitude x treatment interaction (ATI) as a conceptual framework for complementary and alternative medicine outcome research. Part 1—What is ATI research? *The Journal of Alternative and Complementary Medicine, 10*(3), 580–586.

Chen, C., Lee, S., & Stevenson, H. W. (1996). Academic achievement and motivation of Chinese students: A cross-national perspective. In S. Lau (Ed.), *Growing up the Chinese way: Chinese child and adolescent development* (pp. 69–91). Hong Kong: Chinese University Press.

Cheng, K. (2011). Shanghai: How a big city in a developing country leaped to the head of the class. In M. S. Tucker (Ed.), *Surpassing Shanghai: An agenda for American education built on the world's leading systems* (pp. 21–50). Cambridge, MA: Harvard Education Press.

Chingos, M. M., & Peterson, P. E. (2013). The impact of school vouchers on college enrollment. *Education Next, 13*(3), 59–64.

Chingos, M. M., & Peterson, P. E. (2015). Experimentally estimated impacts of school vouchers on college enrollment and degree attainment. *Journal of Public Economics, 122*, 1–12.

Cizek, G. J., & Burg, S. S. (2006). *Addressing test anxiety in a high-stakes environment: Strategies for classrooms and schools*. Thousand Oaks, CA: Corwin.

Claro, S., Paunesku, D., & Dweck, C. S. (2016). Growth mindset tempers the effects of poverty on academic achievement. *Proceedings of the National Academy of Sciences, 113*(31), 8664–8668.

Coleman, J. S., Campbell, E. Q., Hobson, C. J., McPartland, F., Mood, A. M., Weinfeld, F. D., & York, R. L. (1966). *Equality of educational opportunity*. Washington, DC: U.S. Government Printing Office.

Coles, G. (2003). *Reading the naked truth: Literacy, legislation, and lies*. Portsmouth, NH: Heinemann.

Corno, L., Cronbach, L. J., Kupermintz, H., Lohman, D. F., Mandinach, E. B., Porteus, A. W., & Talbert, J. E. (2001). *Remaking the concept of aptitude: Extending the legacy of Richard E. Snow*. New York, NY: Routledge.

Cotter, K. N., Pretz, J. E., & Kaufman, J. C. (2016). Applicant extracurricular involvement predicts creativity better than traditional admissions factors. *Psychology of Aesthetics, Creativity, and the Arts, 10*(1), 2–13.

Coughlan, S. (2012, May 8). China: The world's cleverest country? Retrieved from www.bbc.co.uk/news/business-17585201

Cowen, J. M. (2008). School choice as a latent variable: Estimating the "complier average causal effect" of vouchers in Charlotte. *Policy Studies Journal, 36*(2), 301–315.

Crane, J. (1996). Effects of home environment, SES, and maternal test scores on mathematics achievement. *The Journal of Educational Research, 89*(5), 305–314.

Credé, M., Tynan, M. C., & Harms, P. D. (2017). Much ado about grit: A meta-analytic synthesis of the grit literature. *Journal of Personality and Social Psychology, 113*(3), 492–511.

Cronbach, L. J. (1957). The two disciplines of scientific psychology. *American Psychologist, 12*(11), 671–684.

Cronbach, L. J. (1975). Beyond the two disciplines of scientific psychology. *American Psychologist, 30*, 116–127.

Cronbach, L. J., & Snow, R. E. (1981). *Aptitudes and instructional methods: A handbook for research on interactions.* New York, NY: Irvington.

Cummins, J. (2007). Pedagogies for the poor? Realigning reading instruction for low-income students with scientifically based reading research. *Educational Researcher, 36*(9), 564–572.

Darling-Hammond, L. (2010). *The flat world and education: How America's commitment to equity will determine our future.* New York, NY: Teachers College Press.

Darling-Hammond, L., & Lieberman, A. (Eds.). (2012). *Teacher education around the world.* New York, NY: Routledge.

Dean, D., Jr., & Kuhn, D. (2007). Direct instruction vs. discovery: The long view. *Science Education, 91*(3), 384–397.

Dee, T. S., & Jacob, B. A. (2010). *The impact of No Child Left Behind on students, teachers, and schools.* Washington, DC: Brookings Institute. Retrieved from www.brookings.edu/bpea-articles/the-impact-of-no-child-left-behind-on-students-teachers-and-schools-with-comments-and-discussion/

Dee, T. S., & Jacob, B. (2011). The impact of No Child Left Behind on student achievement. *Journal of Policy Analysis and Management, 30*(3), 418–446.

Dewey, J. (1975). *Democracy and education: An introduction to the philosophy of education.* New York, NY: Free Press.

Dillion, S. (2010, December 7). Top test scores from Shanghai stun educators. *The New York Times.* Retrieved from www.nytimes.com/2010/12/07/education/07education.html

Domina, T., & Penner, E. K. (2013). *Distributional effects of a school voucher program: Evidence from New York City.* Retrieved from emilykpenner.com/epkwp/wp-content/uploads/2013/07/Bitler_Domina_Penner_Hoynes_2013_NYC_Voucher.pdf

Duckworth, A. L., Peterson, C., Matthews, M. D., & Kelly, D. R. (2007). Grit: Perseverance and passion for long-term goals. *Journal of Personality and Social Psychology, 92*(6), 1087–1101.

Duckworth, A. L., & Yeager, D. S. (2015). Measurement matters: Assessing personal qualities other than cognitive ability for educational purposes. *Educational Researcher, 44*(4), 237–251.

Duncan, G. J., & Murnane, R. J. (Eds.). (2011). *Whither opportunuty? Rising inequality, schools, and children's life chances.* New York, NY/Chicago, IL: Russell Sage Foundation/Spencer Foundation.

Dweck, C. S. (1999). *Self-theories: Their role in motivation, personality, and development.* Philadelphia, PA: Psychology Press.

Dweck, C. S. (2006). *Mindset: The new psychology of success.* New York, NY: Random House.

Dynarski, M. (2016). *On negative effects of vouchers.* Retrieved from www.brookings .edu/research/on-negative-effects-of-vouchers/

Ebmeier, H., & Good, T. L. (1979). The effects of instructing teachers about good teaching on the mathematics achievement of fourth grade students. *American Educational Research Journal, 16*(1), 1–16.

Engelmann, S. (2007). *Teaching needy kids in our backward system: 42 years of trying.* Eugene, OR: NIFDI Press.

Espenshade, T. J., & Radford, A. W. (2009). *No longer separate, not yet equal: Race and class in elite college admission and campus life.* Princeton, NJ: Princeton University Press.

Evans, D. (2012, September 14). He's not the messiah. *TES.* Retrieved from www .tes.com/news/tes-archive/tes-publication/hes-not-messiah

Evers, W. M. (Ed.). (1998). *What's gone wrong in America's classrooms.* Palo Alto, CA: Hoover Press.

Every Student Succeeds Act, 114-95, Congress. (2015).

Feniger, Y., & Lefstein, A. (2014). How *not* to reason with PISA data: An ironic investigation. *Journal of Education Policy, 29*(6), 845–855.

Figazzolo, L. (2009). *Impact of PISA 2006 on the education policy debate.* Retrieved from download.ei-ie.org/docs/IRISDocuments/Research Website Documents/2009-00036-01-E.pdf

Flesch, R. (1955). *Why Johnny can't read: And what you can do about it.* New York, NY: Harper Collins.

Florida, R. (2002). *The rise of the creative class . . . and how it's transforming work, leisure, community & everyday life.* New York, NY: Basic Books.

Florida, R. (2012). *The rise of the creative class, revisited* (2nd ed.). New York, NY: Basic Books.

Ford, D. Y., & Grantham, T. C. (2003). Providing access for culturally diverse gifted students: From deficit to dynamic thinking. *Theory into Practice, 42*(3), 217–225.

Forster, G. (2016). *A win-win solution: The empirical evidence on school choice.* Retrieved from www.edchoice.org/wp-content/uploads/2016/05/2016-5-Win -Win-Solution-WEB.pdf

Fowler, F. C. (2002). Introduction: The great school choice debate. *The Clearing House, 76*(1), 4–7.

Freedman, S. G. (2004, October 20). The class multiplies, but the math divides. Retrieved from www.nytimes.com/2004/10/20/education/the-class-multiplies-but -the-math-divides.html

Friedman, M. (1955). *The role of government in education*: New Brunswick, NJ: Rutgers University Press.

Fryer, R. G., & Levitt, S. D. (2004). Understanding the black–white test score gap in the first two years of school. *The Review of Economics and Statistics, 86*(2), 447–464.

Fuchs, L. S., Schumacher, R. F., Sterba, S. K., Long, J., Namkung, J., Malone, A., . . . Siegler, R. S. (2014). Does working memory moderate the effects of fraction intervention? An aptitude–treatment interaction. *Journal of Educational Psychology, 106*(2), 499–514.

Fuller, B. F., & Elmore, R. (1996). *Who chooses? Who loses? Culture, institutions and the unequal effects of school choice.* New York, NY: Teachers College Press.

Fyfe, E. R., Rittle-Johnson, B., & DeCaro, M. S. (2012). The effects of feedback during exploratory mathematics problem solving: Prior knowledge matters. *Journal of Educational Psychology, 104*(4), 1094–1108.

Gagné, R. M. (1968). Learning hierarchies. *Educational Psychologist, 6*(1), 1–9.

Gajda, A., Beghetto, R. A., & Karwowski, M. (2017). Exploring creative learning in the classroom: A multi-method approach. *Thinking Skills and Creativity, 24*, 250–267.

Gamse, B. C., Bloom, H. S., Kemple, J. J., & Jacob, R. T. (2008). *Reading First impact study: Interim report* (NCEE 2008-4016). Retrieved from ies.ed.gov/ncee/pdf/20084016.pdf

Gamse, B. C., Jacob, R. T., Horst, M., Boulay, B., & Unlu, F. (2008). *Reading First impact study: Final report* (NCEE 2009-4038). Retrieved from ies.ed.gov/ncee/pdf/20094038.pdf

Gao, G. (2003). Encountering American education. *Beijing Wenxue*, pp. 6–35.

Gardner, H. (1983). *Frames of mind: The theory of multiple intelligences.* New York, NY: Basic Books.

Gardner, H. (1993). *Multiple intelligences: The theory in practice.* New York, NY: Basic Books.

Gersten, R., & Keating, T. (1987). Long-term benefits from direct instruction. *Educational Leadership, 44*(6), 28–31.

Ginder, S. A., Kelly-Reid, J. E., & Mann, F. B. (2017). *Graduation rates for selected cohorts, 2007–12; student financial aid, academic year 2014–15; and admissions in postsecondary institutions, Fall 2015.* Retrieved from nces.ed.gov/pubs2017/2017084.pdf

Ginsberg, R., & Kingston, N. (2014). Caught in a vise: The challenges facing teacher preparation in an era of accountability. *Teachers College Record, 116*(1). Retrieved from www.tcrecord.org/Content.asp?ContentId=17295

Glod, M. (2008, May 2). Study questions "No Child" Act's reading plan. Retrieved from www.washingtonpost.com/wp-dyn/content/article/2008/05/01/AR2008050101399.html?hpid=sec-education

Goleman, D. (1995). *Emotional intelligence.* New York, NY: Bantam Books.

Gorard, S. (1999). "Well. That about wraps it up for school choice research": A state of the art review. *School Leadership & Management, 19*(1), 25–47.

Gove, M. (2010, December 28). My revolution for culture in classroom: Why we must raise education standards so children can compete with rest of the world. *The Telegraph*. Retrieved from www.telegraph.co.uk/education/8227535/Michael -Gove-my-revolution-for-culture-in-classroom.html

Gray, W. S. (1960). *On their own in reading* (Rev. ed.). Chicago, IL: Scott, Foresman. (Original work published 1948)

Greene, J. P. (2011). *Why America needs school choice*. New York, NY: Encounter Books.

Grissom, J. A., Nicholson-Crotty, S., & Harrington, J. R. (2014). Estimating the effects of No Child Left Behind on teachers' work environments and job attitudes. *Educational Evaluation and Policy Analysis, 36*(4), 417–436.

Gronqvist, E., & Vlachos, J. (2008). *One size fits all? The effects of teacher cognitive and non-cognitive abilities on student achievement*. Retrieved from papers.ssrn.com/sol3/papers.cfm?abstract_id=1311222

Grunwald, M. (2006, October 1). A textbook case: Billions for an inside game on reading. Retrieved from www.washingtonpost.com/wp-dyn/content/article /2006/09/29/AR2006092901333.html

Gunn, B., Biglan, A., Smolkowski, K., & Ary, D. (2000). The efficacy of supplemental instruction in decoding skills for Hispanic and non-Hispanic students in early elementary school. *Journal of Special Education, 34*(2), 90–103.

Hannas, W. C. (2003). *The writing on the wall: How Asian orthography curbs creativity*. Philadelphia: University of Pennsylvania Press.

Hansen, M. (2013). *Right-sizing the classroom: Making the most of great teachers*. Washington, DC: Thomas B. Fordham Institute.

Harris, D. N., & Herrington, C. D. (2006, February). Accountability, standards, and the growing achievement gap: Lessons from the past half-century. *American Journal of Education, 112*(2), 209–238.

Hattie, J. (2008). *Visible learning: A synthesis of over 800 meta-analyses relating to achievement*. New York, NY: Routledge.

Hattie, J. (2012). *Visible learning for teachers: Maximizing impact on learning*. New York, NY: Routledge.

Hattie, J. (2015). The applicability of visible learning to higher education. *Scholarship of Teaching and Learning in Psychology, 1*(1), 79–91.

Hess, F. M. (2011, Fall). Our achievement-gap mania. *National Affairs, 9*, 113–129.

Hess, F. M., & Petrilli, M. J. (2004). The politics of No Child Left Behind: Will the coalition hold? *The Journal of Education, 185*(3), 13–25.

Hess, F. M., & Rotherham, A. J. (2007). NCLB and the competitiveness agenda: Happy collaboration or a collision course? *Phi Delta Kappan, 88*(5), 345–352.

Hirsch, E. D., Jr. (2010, May 13). How to save the schools. *The New York Review of Books*. Retrieved from www.nybooks.com/articles/2010/05/13/how-save -schools/

Ho, E. S. C. (2003). Accomplishment and challenges of Hong Kong education system: What we have learned from PISA. *Educational Journal, 31*(2), 1–30.

Hornickel, J., Zecker, S. G., Bradlow, A. R., & Kraus, N. (2012). Assistive listening devices drive neuroplasticity in children with dyslexia. *Proceedings of the National Academy of Sciences, 109*(41), 16731–16736.

House, E., Glass, G., McLean, L., & Walker, D. F. (1978). No simple answer: Critique of the Follow Through evaluation. *Harvard Educational Review, 48*(2), 128–160.

Hout, M., & Elliott, S. W. (Eds.). (2011). *Incentives and test-based accountability in education*. Washington, DC: National Academies Press.

Howell, W. G., & Peterson, P. E. (2006). *The education gap: Vouchers and urban schools*. Washington, DC: Brookings Institution Press.

HSBC. (2017). *The value of education: Higher and higher* (Global report). Retrieved from www.hsbc.com/-/media/hsbc-com/newsroomassets/2017/pdfs/170628-the -value-of-education-higher-and-higher-global-report.pdf

Hu, W. (2010, October 1). Making math lessons as easy as 1, pause, 2, pause . . . *The New York Times*, p. A1. Retrieved from www.nytimes.com/2010/10/01 /education/01math.html

Huicong Net. (2005, November 23). Diaocha: 13.3% Zhejiang zhongxiao xueshen cheng jihua zisha [Study: 13.3% students in Zhejian considered suicide]. Retrieved from info.edu.hc360.com/2005/11/23141185758.shtml

Janicki, T. C., & Peterson, P. L. (1981). Aptitude-treatment interaction effects of variations in direct instruction. *American Educational Research Journal, 18*(1), 63–82.

Janssen, W. F. (1981). The story of the laws behind the labels. Retrieved from www. fda.gov/aboutfda/whatwedo/history/overviews/ucm056044.htm

Jencks, C., & Phillips, M. (Eds.). (1998). *The black–white test score gap*. Washington, DC: Brookings Institute Press.

Jennings, J. L., & Bearak, J. M. (2014). "Teaching to the test" in the NCLB era: How test predictability affects our understanding of student performance. *Educational Researcher, 43*(8), 381–389.

Jennings, J., & Rentner, D. S. (2006). Ten big effects of the No Child Left Behind Act on public schools. *Phi Delta Kappan, 88*(2), 110–113.

Jensen, B. (2012). *Catching up: Learning from the best school systems in East Asia*. Retrieved from grattan.edu.au/report/catching-up-learning-from-the-best -school-systems-in-east-asia/

Jiang, X. (2010, December 8). The test Chinese schools still fail: High scores for Shanghai's 15-year-olds are actually a sign of weakness. *The Wall Street Journal*. Retrieved from www.wsj.com/articles/SB10001424052748703766704576 008692493038646

Jin, H., Barnard, J., & Rubin, D. B. (2010). A modified general location model for noncompliance with missing data: Revisiting the New York City School Choice Scholarship Program using principal stratification. *Journal of Educational and Behavioral Statistics, 35*(2), 154–173.

Jing, L. (2015, November 26). Study shows Chinese students spend three hours on homework per day. *China Daily*. Retrieved from www.chinadaily.com.cn/china /2015-11/26/content_22520832.htm

John, O. P., Robins, R. W., & Pervin, L. A. (2008). *Handbook of personality: Theory and research* (3rd ed.). New York, NY: Guilford Press.

Jones, L. (2013). *Minding the gap: A rhetorical history of the achievement gap* (Doctoral dissertation). Louisiana State University, Baton Rouge, LA. Retrieved from digitalcommons.lsu.edu/gradschool_dissertations/3633/

Kamenetz, A. (2014, October 11). It's 2014. All children are supposed to be proficient. What happened? *NPR.* Retrieved from www.npr.org/sections/ed/2014/10/11/354931351/it-s-2014-all-children-are-supposed-to-be-proficient-under-federal-law

Kaplan, K. (2016, December 9). Cooling cap helps cancer patients preserve their hair during chemotherapy, clinical trial shows. *The Los Angeles Times.* Retrieved from www.latimes.com/science/sciencenow/la-sci-sn-cooling-scalp-chemotherapy-20161209-story.html

Kapur, M. (2014). Productive failure in learning math. *Cognitive Science, 38*(5), 1008–1022.

Kapur, M. (2016). Examining productive failure, productive success, unproductive failure, and unproductive success in learning. *Educational Psychologist, 51*(2), 289–299.

Kapur, M., & Bielaczyc, K. (2012). Designing for productive failure. *Journal of the Learning Sciences, 21*(1), 45–83.

Kennedy, M. M. (1978). Findings from the Follow Through planned variation study. *Educational Researcher, 7*(6), 3–11.

Kennedy, M. M. (1991). Policy issues in teacher education. *Phi Delta Kappan, 72*(9), 658–665.

Kern, M. L., & Friedman, H. S. (2009). Early educational milestones as predictors of lifelong academic achievement, midlife adjustment, and longevity. *Journal of Applied Developmental Psychology, 30*(4), 419–430.

Kieft, M., Rijlaarsdam, G., & van den Bergh, H. (2008). An aptitude–treatment interaction approach to writing-to-learn. *Learning and Instruction, 18*(4), 379–390.

Kim, J. S. (2008). Research and the reading wars. In F. M. Hess (Ed.), *When research matters: How scholarship influences education policy* (pp. 89–112). Cambridge, MA: Harvard Education Press.

Kim, J., & Kim, Y. (2014, May 11). True lessons of East Asian education. Retrieved from www.huffingtonpost.com/jungkyu-kim/true-lessons-of-east-asia-education_b_4932423.html

Kim, K. (2010). An international comparsion of Korean student achievement on the PISA and TIMSS. In C. J. Lee, S. Kim, & D. Adams (Eds.), *Sixty years of Korean education* (pp. 259–284). Seoul, Korea: Seoul National University Press.

Kim, K. H. (2005). Learning from each other: Creativity in East Asian and American education. *Creativity Research Journal, 17*(4), 337–347.

Kim, T., & Axelrod, S. (2005). Direct instruction: An educators' guide and a plea for action. *The Behavior Analyst Today, 6*(2), 111–120.

Klahr, D., & Nigam, M. (2004). The equivalence of learning paths in early science instruction: Effects of direct instruction and discovery learning. *Psychological Science, 15*(10), 661–667.

Klein, D. (2003). A brief history of American K–12 mathematics education in the 20th century. In J. Royer (Ed.), *Mathematical cognition* (pp. 175–225). Charlotte, NC: Information Age.

Klein, D. (2007). A quarter century of US 'math wars' and political partisanship. *BSHM Bulletin: Journal of the British Society for the History of Mathematics, 22*(1), 22–33.

Kline, M. (1973). *Why Johnny can't add: The failure of the new math.* New York, NY: St. Martin's Press.

Knudson, K. (2015, September 9). The common core is today's new math—which is actually a good thing. *The Conversation.* Retrieved from theconversation.com /the-common-core-is-todays-new-math-which-is-actually-a-good-thing-46585

Koreman, S., & Winship, C. (2000). A reanalysis of the bell curve: Intelligence, family background, and schooling. In K. Arrow, S. Bowles, & S. Durlauf (Eds.), *Meritocracy and economic inequality* (pp. 137–178). Princeton, NJ: Princeton University Press.

Krathwohl, D. R. (2002). A revision of Bloom's taxonomy: An overview. *Theory into Practice, 41*(4), 212–218.

Kreiner, S., & Christensen, K. B. (2014, April). Analyses of model fit and robustness. A new look at the PISA scaling model underlying ranking of countries according to reading literacy. *Psychometrika.* doi:10.1007/s11336-013-9347-z

Krieg, J. M. (2008). Are students left behind? The distributional effects of the No Child Left Behind Act. *Education, 3*(2), 250–281.

Kristof, N. D. (2011, January 15). China's winning schools? *New York Times.* Retrieved from www.nytimes.com/2011/01/16/opinion/16kristof.html

Krueger, A. B., Hanushek, E. A., & Rice, J. K. (2002). *The class size debate.* Washington, DC: Economic Policy Institute.

Krueger, A. B., & Zhu, P. (2004). Another look at the New York City school voucher experiment. *American Behavioral Scientist, 47*(5), 658–698.

Labaree, D. F. (1997). Public goods, private goods: The American struggle over educational goals. *American Educational Research Journal, 34*(1), 39–81.

Ladd, H. F. (2017). No Child Left Behind: A deeply flawed federal policy. *Journal of Policy Analysis and Management, 36*(2), 461–469.

Ladd, H. F., & Lauen, D. L. (2010). Status versus growth: The distributional effects of school accountability policies. *Journal of Policy Analysis and Management, 29*(3), 426–450.

Ladson-Billings, G. (2006). From the achievement gap to the education debt: Understanding achievement in U.S. schools. *Educational Researcher, 35*(7), 3–12.

Ladson-Billings, G. (2007). Pushing past the achievement gap: An essay on the language of deficit. *The Journal of Negro Education, 76*(3), 316–323.

Lamb, S., & Fullarton, S. (2002). Classroom and school factors affecting mathematics achievement: A comparative study of Australia and the United States using TIMSS. *Australian Journal of Education, 46*(2), 154–171.

Larson, M. (2017, February 20). The elusive search for balance. Retrieved from www.nctm.org/News-and-Calendar/Messages-from-the-President/Archive/ Matt-Larson/The-Elusive-Search-for-Balance/

Leung, F.K.S. (2002). Behind the high achievement of East Asian students. *Educational Research and Evaluation: An International Journal on Theory and Practice, 8*(1), 87–108.

Levin, H. M. (2012). More than just test scores. *Prospects: The Quarterly Review of Comparative Education, 42*(3), 269–284.

Li, J. (2013, January 15). Beyond the grades. *The Standard.* Retrieved from www.thestandard.com.hk/news_detail.asp?we_cat=16&art_id=130084&sid=38696570&con_type=1&d_str=20130115&fc=4

Lin, J. Y. (2006, December). *Needham puzzle, Weber question and China's miracle: Long-term performance since the Sung Dynasty.* Paper presented at World Economic Performance: Past, Present and Future—Long Term Performance and Prospects of Australia and Major Asian Economies, Brisbane, Australia. Retrieved from www.uq.edu.au/economics/cepa/docs/seminar/papers-nov2006/Lin-Paper.pdf

Linn, R. L., Baker, E. L., & Betebenner, D. W. (2002). Accountability systems: Implications of requirements of the No Child Left Behind Act of 2001. *Educational Researcher, 31*(6), 3–16.

Loveless, T. (2006a). *How well are American students learning?* Retrieved from www.brookings.edu/research/the-2006-brown-center-report-on-american-education-how-well-are-american-students-learning/

Loveless, T. (2006b, August 1). *The peculiar politics of No Child Left Behind.* Washington, DC: Brookings Institution. Retrieved from www.brookings.edu/research/the-peculiar-politics-of-no-child-left-behind/

Loveless, T. (2014). *PISA's China problem continues: A response to Schleicher, Zhang, and Tucker.* Retrieved from www.brookings.edu/research/papers/2014/01/08-shanghai-pisa-loveless

Lubienski, C. (2016). Review of *A win-win solution* and *The participant effects of private school vouchers across the globe.* Retrieved from nepc.colorado.edu/files/reviews/TTR Lubienski Meta-Analysis.pdf

Mansell, W. (2008, November 21). Research reveals teaching's holy grail. *TES.* Retrieved from www.tes.com/news/tes-archive/tes-publication/research-reveals-teachings-holy-grail

Manzo, K. K. (2007, May 9). Senate report details "Reading First" conflicts of interest. Retrieved from www.edweek.org/ew/articles/2007/05/09/37read_web.h26.html

Manzo, K. K. (2008a, March 12). Directors of "Reading First" plagued by anxiety over budget cuts. *Education Week,* pp. 20, 22. Retrieved from www.edweek.org/ew/articles/2008/03/12/27read.h27.html

Manzo, K. K. (2008b, December 3). Federal path for reading questioned: "Reading First" poor results offer limited guidance. *Education Week,* pp. 1, 16–17. Retrieved from www.edweek.org/ew/articles/2008/12/03/14read_ep.h28.html

Martin, B. J. (2014). *Elixir: The American tragedy of a deadly drug.* Lancaster, PA: Barkerry Press.

McKinsey & Company. (2007). *How the world's best-performing school systems come out on top*. Retrieved from www.mckinsey.com/industries/social-sector/our-insights/how-the-worlds-best-performing-school-systems-come-out-on-top

McKinsey & Company. (2009). *The economic impact of the achievement gap in America's schools*. Retrieved from dropoutprevention.org/wp-content/uploads/2015/07/ACHIEVEMENT_GAP_REPORT_20090512.pdf

McLaren, M., & Brown, E. (2017, July 15). Trump wants to spend millions more on school vouchers. But what's happened to the millions already spent? *The Washington Post*. Retrieved from www.washingtonpost.com/local/education/trump-wants-to-spend-millions-more-on-school-vouchers-but-whats-happened-to-the-millions-already-spent/2017/07/15/ab6002a8-6267-11e7-84a1-a26b75ad39fe_story.html?utm_term=.2c938636e65e

McMurrer, J. (2007). NCLB year 5: *Choices, changes, and challenges: Curriculum and instruction in the NCLB era*. Retrieved from www.cep-dc.org/displayDocument.cfm?DocumentID=312

Mead, R. (2014, April 30). Louis C.K. against the common core. *The New Yorker*. Retrieved from www.newyorker.com/news/daily-comment/louis-c-k-against-the-common-core

Meadows, M. (2006). Promoting safe and effective drugs for 100 years. *FDA Consumer magazine*. Retrieved from www.fda.gov/AboutFDA/WhatWeDo/History/CentennialofFDA/CentennialEditionofFDAConsumer/ucm093787.htm

Menken, K. (2006). Teaching to the test: How No Child Left Behind impacts language policy, curriculum, and instruction for English language learners. *Bilingual Research Journal, 30*(2), 521–546.

Meroni, E. C., Vera-Toscano, E., & Costa, P. (2015). Can low skill teachers make good students? Empirical evidence from PIAAC and PISA. *Journal of Policy Modeling, 37*(2), 308–323. doi.org/10.1016/j.jpolmod.2015.02.006

Meyer, H.-D., & Benavot, A. (2013). *PISA, power, and policy: The emergence of global educational governance*. Oxford, UK: Oxford University Press.

Meyer, L. A. (1984). Long-term academic effects of the direct instruction project Follow Through. *The Elementary School Journal, 84*(4), 380–394.

Mills, J. N., & Wolf, P. J. (2016). *The effects of the Louisiana Scholarship Program on student achievement after two years*. Retrieved from media.nola.com/education_impact/other/Report 1 - LSP Y2 Achievement - Embargo.pdf

Mishkind, A. (2014). *Overview: State definitions of college and career readiness*. Retrieved from ccrscenter.org/sites/default/files/CCRS Defintions Brief_REV_1.pdf

Mismanagement and conflicts of interest in the Reading First program, U.S. House of Representatives, First Sess. 96 (2007).

Morrison, H. (2013, December 1). Pisa 2012 major flaw exposed. Retrieved from paceni.wordpress.com/2013/12/01/pisa-2012-major-flaw-exposed/

Mullis, I. V. S., Martin, M. O., Beaton, A. E., Gonzalez, E. J., Kelly, D. L., & Smith, T. A. (1997). *Mathematics achievement in the primary school years: IEA's third international mathematics and science study*. Boston, MA: IEA.

Mullis, I. V. S., Martin, M. O., & Foy, P. (2008). *TIMSS 2007 international mathematics report: Findings from IEA's trends in international mathematics and science study at the fourth and eighth grades.* Retrieved from timss.bc.edu/TIMSS2007/mathreport.html

Mullis, I. V. S., Martin, M. O., Foy, P., & Arora, A. (2012). *TIMSS 2011 international results in mathematics.* Retrieved from timssandpirls.bc.edu/timss2011/international-results-mathematics.html

Mullis, I. V. S., Martin, M. O., & Loveless, T. (2016). *20 Years of TIMSS: International trends in mathematics and science: Achievement, curriculum, and instruction.* Retrieved from timssandpirls.bc.edu/timss2015/international-results/timss2015/wp-content/uploads/2016/T15-20-years-of-TIMSS.pdf

National Assessment of Educational Progress (NAEP). (2015). 2015 mathematics & reading assessments. Retrieved from www.nationsreportcard.gov/reading_math_2015/#?grade=8

National Center for Education Statistics. (1999). *Highlights from TIMSS.* Retrieved from nces.ed.gov/pubs99/1999081.pdf

National Center for Education Statistics. (2012). *NAEP 2012: Trends in academic progress: Reading 1971–2012 | Mathematics 1973–2012.* Retrieved from nces.ed.gov/nationsreportcard/subject/publications/main2012/pdf/2013456.pdf

National Center for Education Statistics. (2017). Common core of data: Data tables. Retrieved from nces.ed.gov/ccd/data_tables.asp

National Defense Education Act of 1958, Pub. L. No. 85-864 (1958).

National Education Association. (2011). Reading yesterday and today: The NRP report and other factors. Retrieved from www.nea.org/readingupdates

National Governors Association Center for Best Practices, & Council of Chief State School Officers. (2010). *Common Core State Standards.* Retrieved from www.corestandards.org/

National Institute for Direct Instruction. (2014). *Achieving success for every student with direct instruction.* Eugene, OR: NIFDI Press.

National Institute for Direct Instruction. (2015). *Writings on direct instruction: A bibliography.* Retrieved from www.nifdi.org/docman/research/bibliography/205-di-bibliography-reference-list/file

National Institute for Direct Instruction. (2017). Basic philosophy of direct instruction (DI). Retrieved from www.nifdi.org/what-is-di/basic-philosophy

National Institute of Child Health and Human Development. (2000a). National Reading Panel. Retrieved from www.nichd.nih.gov/research/supported/Pages/nrp.aspx

National Institute of Child Health and Human Development. (2000b). *Teaching children to read: An evidence-based assessment of the scientific research literature on reading and its implications for reading instruction: Report of the Subgroups.* Washington, DC: Author.

National Institute of Child Health and Human Development. (2000c). *Teaching children to read: An evidence-based assessment of the scientific research literature on reading and its implications for reading instruction: Summary.* Washington, DC: Author.

National Mathematics Advisory Panel. (2008). *Foundations for success: The final report of the National Mathematics Advisory Panel.* Washington, DC: U.S. Department of Education.

National Research Council. (1999). *Global perspectives for local action: Using TIMSS to improve U.S. mathematics and science education.* Washington, DC: National Academy Press.

Neal, D., & Schanzenbach, D. W. (2010). Left behind by design: Proficiency counts and test-based accountability. *The Review of Economics and Statistics, 92*(2), 263–283.

Needham, J. (Ed.). (1954). *Science and civilisation in China.* Cambridge, UK: University of Cambridge Press.

Nelson, D. I. (2002). *Using TIMSS to inform policy and practice at the local level* (CPRE Policy Brief No. 36). Retrieved from www.cpre.org/using-timss-inform-policy-and-practice-local-level

Nichols, S. L., & Berliner, D. C. (2007). *Collateral damage: How high-stakes testing corrupts America's schools.* Cambridge, MA: Harvard Education Press.

Nicotera, A., & Stuit, D. (2017). *Three signs that a proposed charter school is at risk of failing.* Washington, DC: Thomas B. Fordham Institute.

No Child Left Behind Act of 2001, 107-110, Congress (2002).

Norris, N. D. (2004). *The promise and failure of progressive education.* London, UK: Scarecrow Education.

Obama, B. (2015, December 10). Remarks by the president at Every Student Succeeds Act signing ceremony. Retrieved from obamawhitehouse.archives.gov/the-press-office/2015/12/10/remarks-president-every-student-succeeds-act-signing-ceremony

Odum, E. P. (1997). *Ecology: A bridge between science and society.* Sunderland, MA: Sinauer Associates.

OECD. (2011). *Strong performers and successful reformers in education: Lessons from PISA for the United States.* Retrieved from dx.doi.org/10.1787/9789264096660-en

OECD. (2013). *Ready to learn: Students' engagement, drive and self-beliefs.* Retrieved from www.oecd.org/pisa/keyfindings/pisa-2012-results-volume-III.pdf

OECD. (2014). *PISA 2012 results: What students know and can do: Student performance in mathematics, reading and science (Volume I) [Revised edition February 2014].* Retrieved from www.oecd.org/pisa/keyfindings/pisa-2012-results-volume-i.htm

OECD. (2016). *PISA 2015 results (Volume I): Excellence and equity in Education.* Retrieved from dx.doi.org/10.1787/9789264266490-en

OECD. (2017). *PISA 2015 results: Students' well-being.* Retrieved from www.oecd.org/education/pisa-2015-results-volume-iii-9789264273856-en.htm

Office of Inspector General. (2006). *The Reading First program's grant application process: Final inspection report.* Retrieved from www2.ed.gov/about/offices/list/oig/aireports/i13f0017.pdf

Page, S. E. (2007). *The difference: How the power of diversity creates better groups, firms, schools and societies.* Princeton, NJ: Princeton University Press.

Paige, R., & Whitty, E. (2010). *The black–white achievement gap: Why closing it is the greatest civil rights issue of our time.* New York, NY: AMACOM.

Pak, H. B. (1974). *China and the West: Myths and realities in history.* Leiden, Netherlands: E. J. Brill.

Partnership for 21st Century Skills. (2007). *Framework for 21st century learning.* Retrieved from www.p21.org/our-work/p21-framework

Pearson, P. D. (1989). Reading the whole-language movement. *The Elementary School Journal, 90*(2), 231–241.

Pearson, P. D. (2004). The reading wars. *Educational Policy, 18*(1), 216–252.

Peterson, P. L. (1979). Direct instruction: Effective for what and for whom. *Educational Leadership, 37*(1), 46–48.

Phillips, C. J. (2015, February 11). The new math strikes back. Retrieved from time .com/3694171/the-new-math-strikes-back/

PISA. (2003). *First results from PISA 2003.* Retrieved from www.oecd.org/dataoecd /1/63/34002454.pdf

PISA. (2007). *PISA 2006: Advance details.* Retrieved from www.oecd.org/document /40/0,3343,en_32252351_32235731_39701864_1_1_1_1,00.html

Plucker, J. A., Burroughs, N., & Song, R. (2010). *Mind the (other) gap: The growing excellence gap in K–12 education.* Retrieved from files.eric.ed.gov /fulltext/ED531840.pdf

Plucker, J. A., Hardesty, J., & Burroughs, N. (2013). *Talents on the sidelines: Excellence gaps and America's persistent talent underclass.* Retrieved from webdev.education.uconn.edu/static/sites/cepa/AG/excellence2013/Excellence -Gap-10-18-13_JP_LK.pdf

Pretz, J. E., & Kaufman, J. C. (2015). Do traditional admissions criteria reflect applicant creativity? *The Journal of Creative Behavior 51*(3), 240–251.

Qin, A. (2017, August 6). Britain turns to Chinese textbooks to improve its math scores. *The New York Times,* p. 48. Retrieved from www.nytimes .com/2017/08/05/world/asia/china-textbooks-britain.html?_r=0

Ravitch, D. (2001). *Left back: A century of battles over school reform.* New York, NY: Simon & Schuster.

Ravitch, D. (2010). *The death and life of the great American school system: How testing and choice are undermining education.* New York, NY: Basic Books.

Ravitch, D. (2013). *Reign of error: The hoax of the privatization movement and the danger to America's public schools.* New York, NY: Knopf.

Ravitch, D. (2015, April 2). The lost purpose of school reform. *The New York Review of Books.* Retrieved from www.nybooks.com/daily/2015/04/02/lost -purpose-no-child-left-behind/

Reardon, S. F. (2011). The widening academic achievement gap between the rich and the poor: New evidence and possible explanations. In G. J. Duncan & R. J. Murnane (Eds.), *Whither opportunuty? Rising inequality, schools, and children's life chances* (pp. 91–116). New York, NY/Chicago, IL: Russell Sage Foundation/Spencer Foundation.

Reback, R., Rockoff, J. E., & Schwartz, H. L. (2010). *The effects of No Child Left Behind on school services and student outcomes.* Retrieved from citeseerx.ist .psu.edu/viewdoc/download?doi=10.1.1.550.8539&rep=rep1&type=pdf

Reback, R., Rockoff, J., & Schwartz, H. L. (2011). Under pressure: Job security, resource allocation, and productivity in schools under NCLB (NBER working paper no. 16745). Retrieved from www.nber.org/papers/w16745

Reeves, R. V., & Halikias, D. (2017). *Race gaps in SAT scores highlight inequality and hinder upward mobility.* Retrieved from www.brookings.edu/research /race-gaps-in-sat-scores-highlight-inequality-and-hinder-upward-mobility/

Reiss, S. (2004). Multifaceted nature of intrinsic motivation: The theory of 16 basic desires. *Review of General Psychology, 8*(3), 179–183.

Reiss, S. (2008). *The normal personality: A new way of thinking about people.* New York, NY: Cambridge University Press.

Rice, J. K. (2003). *Teacher quality: Understanding the effectiveness of teacher attributes.* Washington, DC: Economic Policy Institute.

Ridley, M. (2003). *Nature via nurture: Genes, experience, and what makes us human.* New York, NY: HarperCollins.

Riley, R. W. (1998). The state of mathematics education: Building a strong foundation for the 21st century. *Notice of the American Mathematical Society, 45*(4), 487–491.

Roehler, L. R., & Duffy, G. G. (1982). Matching direct instruction to reading outcomes. *Language Arts, 59*(5), 476–480.

Rosales, J. (2015, December 15). Closing schools: Privatization disguised as "accountability." *NEA Today.* Retrieved from neatoday.org/2015/12/15/closing -schools-privatization/

Rose, L. C., & Gallup, A. M. (2002, September). *The 34th annual Phi Delta Kappa/ Gallup poll of the public's attitudes toward the public schools.* Retrieved from www.pdkmembers.org/members_online/publications/GallupPoll/kpoll_pdfs /pdkpoll34_2002.pdf

Rose, T. (2016). *The end of average: How we succeed in a world that values sameness.* New York, NY: HarperOne.

Rosenshine, B. V. (1978). Academic engaged time, content covered, and direct instruction. *The Journal of Education, 160*(3), 38–66.

Rosenshine, B. (2008). *Five meanings of direct instruction.* Retrieved from www. centerii.org/search/Resources%5CFiveDirectInstruct.pdf

Rosenshine, B. (2009). The empirical support for direct instruction. In S. Tobias & T. M. Duffy (Eds.), *Constructivist instruction: Success or failure?* (pp. 201–220). New York, NY: Routledge

Rouse, C. E. (1998). Private school vouchers and student achievement: An evaluation of the Milwaukee parental choice program. *The Quarterly Journal of Economics, 113*(2), 553–602.

Royal, C. (2012, November 10). Please stop using the phrase "achievement gap." Retrieved from www.good.is/articles/please-stop-using-the-phrase-achievement-gap

Ryan, R. M., & Deci, E. L. (2017). *Self-determination theory: Basic psychological needs in motivation, development, and wellness*. New York, NY: Guilford Press.

Sahlberg, P. (2017). *FinnishED leadership*. Thousand Oaks, CA: Corwin.

Sanchez, C. (Writer). (2013). *El Paso schools cheating scandal: Who's accountable?* Washington, DC: National Public Radio.

Schleicher, A. (2013, December 3). What we learn from the PISA 2012 results. Retrieved from oecdeducationtoday.blogspot.com/2013/12/what-we-learn-from-pisa-2012-results.html

Schleicher, A. (2016, December 6). Opinion: What Asian schools can teach the rest of us. *CNN*. Retrieved from www.cnn.com/2016/12/06/opinions/education-pisa-rankings-china/index.html

Schmidt, W. H. (1999). Facing the consequences: Using TIMSS for a closer look at U.S. mathematics and science education. Boston, MA: Kluwer Academic.

Schoenfeld, A. H. (2004). The math wars. *Educational Policy, 18*(1), 253–286.

Schweinhart, L. J., & Weikart, D. P. (1997). The High/Scope preschool curriculum comparison study through age 23. *Early Childhood Research Quarterly, 12*(2), 117–143.

Schweinhart, L. J., Weikart, D. P., & Larner, M. B. (1986). Consequences of three preschool curriculum models through age 15. *Early Childhood Research Quarterly, 1*(1), 15–45.

Schwerdt, G., & Wuppermann, A. C. (2011). Sage on the stage: Is lecturing really all that bad? *Education Next, 11*(3), 63–67.

Segool, N. K., Carlson, J. S., Goforth, A. N., Von Der Embse, N., & Barterian, J. A. (2013). Heightened test anxiety among young children: Elementary school students' anxious responses to high-stakes testing. *Psychology in the Schools, 50*(5), 489–499.

Shakeel, M. D., Anderson, K. P., & Wolf, P. J. (2016). *The participant effects of private school vouchers across the globe: A meta-analytic and systematic review*. Retrieved from www.uaedreform.org/downloads/2016/05/the-participant-effects-of-private-school-vouchers-across-the-globe-a-meta-analytic-and-systematic-review-2.pdf

Singapore Ministry of Education. (2012, December 11). International studies affirm Singapore students' strengths in reading, mathematics & science. Retrieved from www.moe.gov.sg/news/press-releases/international-studies-affirm-singapore-students--strengths-in-reading--mathematics-and-science

Sjøberg, S. (2012). PISA: Politics, fundamental problems and intriguing results. *Recherches en Education, 14*. Retrieved from www.recherches-en-education.net/spip.php?article140

Slavin, R. E. (2002). Evidence-based education policies: Transforming educational practice and research. *Educational Researcher, 31*(7), 15–21.

Slavin, R. E. (2008). Cooperative learning, success for all, and evidence-based reform in education. *Éducation et Didactique, 2*(2), 149–157.

Sneader, W. (2005). *Drug discovery: A history*. Hoboken, NJ: Wiley.

Snook, I., O'Neill, J., Clark, J., O'Neill, A.-M., & Openshaw, R. (2009). Invisible learnings? A commentary on John Hattie's book: Visible learning: A synthesis of over 800 meta-analyses relating to achievement. *New Zealand Journal of Educational Studies, 44*(1), 93–106.

Snow, R. E. (1978). Aptitude-treatment interactions in educational research. In L. A. Pervin & M. Lewis (Eds.), *Perspectives in interactional psychology* (pp. 237–262). Boston, MA: Springer.

Snow, R. E. (1991). Aptitude-treatment interaction as a framework for research on individual differences in psychotherapy. *Journal of Consulting and Clinical Psychology, 59*(2), 205–216.

Snow, R. E. (1992). Aptitude theory: Yesterday, today, and tomorrow. *Educational Psychologist, 27*(1), 5–32.

Southgate, D. E. (2009). *Determinants of shadow education: A cross-national analysis* (Doctoral dissertation). The Ohio State University, Columbus, OH. Retrieved from etd.ohiolink.edu/!etd.send_file?accession=osu1259703574&disposition=inline

Stebbins, L. B. (1977). *Education as experimentation: A planned variation model* (Vol. 4). Lanham, MD: University Press of America.

Stephens, T., & Brynner, R. (2009). *Dark remedy: The impact of thalidomide and its revival as a vital medicine.* New York, NY: Basic Books.

Stern, S. (2008). *Too good to last: The true story of Reading First.* Washington, DC: Thomas B. Fordham Institute.

Sternberg, R. J. (1988). *The triarchic mind: A new theory of human intelligence.* New York, NY: Viking Books.

Stevenson, H., & Stigler, J. W. (1994). *The learning gap: Why our schools are failing and what we can learn from Japanese and Chinese education.* New York, NY: Simon & Schuster.

Stevenson, H. W., & Stigler, J. W. (2006). *The learning gap: Why our schools are failing and what we can learn from Japanese and Chinese education* (2nd ed.). New York, NY: Simon & Schuster.

Stewart, W. (2013, December 3). Is Pisa fundamentally flawed? Retrieved from www.tes.co.uk/article.aspx?storycode=6344672

Stockard, J. (2010). Promoting reading achievement and countering the "fourth-grade slump": The impact of direct instruction on reading achievement in fifth grade. *Journal of Education for Students Placed at Risk, 15*(3), 218–240.

Strang, R. (1967). The current status and enduring value of "On their own in reading" by W. S. Gray. *The School Review, 75*(1), 114–121.

Strauss, V. (2011, June 3). 5th grader's essay: High-stakes tests lead to stress, not learning. *The Washington Post.* Retrieved from www.washingtonpost.com/blogs/answer-sheet/post/5th-graders-essay-high-stakes-tests-lead-to-stress-not-learning/2011/06/02/AGQbJIIH_blog.html?utm_term=.775872606047

Success for All Foundation. (2017). Highlights. Results. Retrieved from www.successforall.org/results/

Suicide the leading cause of death among youth. (2007, March 27). *China Daily*. Retrieved from spanish.china.org.cn/english/China/204533.htm

Swanson, H. L., & Sachse-Lee, C. (2000). A meta-analysis of single-subject-design intervention research for students with LD. *Journal of Learning Disabilities, 33*(2), 114–136.

Tarver, S. G. (1998). Myths and truths about direct instruction. *Effective School Practices, 17*(1), 18–22.

Tate, W. F. (1997). Race-ethnicity, SES, gender, and language proficiency trends in mathematics achievement: An update. *Journal for Research in Mathematics Education, 28*(6), 652–679.

Telegraph Reporters. (2016, July 23). Half of primary school pupils to follow Chinese style of learning maths with focus on whole-class teaching. Retrieved from www.telegraph.co.uk/education/2016/07/12/half-of-primary-school-pupils-to-follow-chinese-style-of-learnin/

Terhart, E. (2011). Has John Hattie really found the holy grail of research on teaching? An extended review of visible learning. *Journal of Curriculum Studies, 43*(3), 425–438.

Tienken, C. H. (2008). Rankings of international achievement test performance and economic strength: Correlation or conjecture? *International Journal of Education Policy & Leadership, 3*(4), 1–15.

Tienken, C. H., & Zhao, Y. (2013). How common standards and standardized testing widen the opportunity gap. In P. L. Carter & K. G. Welner (Eds.), *Closing the opportunity gap: What America must do to give every child an even chance* (pp. 113–122). New York, NY: Oxford University Press.

Toppo, G., Amos, D., Gillum, J., & Upton, J. (2011, March 17). When test scores seem too good to believe. *USA Today*. Retrieved from www.usatoday.com/news/education/2011-03-06-school-testing_N.htm

Tu, R., & Lin, R. (2009). Shanghai Chengxiang Jumin Jiating Jiaoyu Zhichu ji Jiaoyu Fudan Zhuangkuan Diaocha Fenxi [A Survey of Family Education Expenditures in Shanghai]. *Jiaoyu fazhan yanjiu [Research in Educational Development], 2009*(21), 21–25.

Tucker, M. (Ed.). (2011). *Surpassing Shanghai: An agenda for American education built on the world's leading systems.* Boston, MA: Harvard Education Press.

Tucker, M. (2014). *Chinese lessons: Shanghai's rise to the top of the PISA league tables.* Retrieved from www.ncee.org/wp-content/uploads/2013/10/ChineseLessonsWeb.pdf

Tucker, M. (2016, February 29). Asian countries take the U.S. to school. *The Atlantic.* Retrieved from www.theatlantic.com/education/archive/2016/02/us-asia-education-differences/471564/

U.S. Department of Education. (2002a). Closing the achievement gap in America's public schools. Retrieved from www.ed.gov/nclb/overview/welcome/closing/index.html

U.S. Department of Education. (2002b). Reading first: Purpose. Retrieved from www2.ed.gov/programs/readingfirst/index.html

U.S. Department of Education. (2002c, March). *Strategic plan 2002–2007*. Retrieved from www2.ed.gov/about/reports/strat/plan2002-07/plan.pdf

U.S. Department of Health and Human Services, Food and Drug Administration, Center for Drug Evaluation and Research, Center for Biologics Evaluation and Research. (2012). *Guidance for industry and investigators: Safety reporting requirements for INDs and BA/BE studies*. Retrieved from www.fda.gov/downloads/Drugs/GuidanceComplianceRegulatoryInformation/Guidances/UCM227351.pdf

Valencia, R. R. (2012). Deficit thinking paradigm. In J. A. Banks (Ed.), *Encyclopedia of diversity in education* (pp. 612–614). Thousand Oaks, CA: Sage.

Valencia, R. R. (2015). *Students of color and the achievement gap: Systematic challenges, systematic transformations*. New York, NY: Routledge, Taylor & Francis Group.

Vinovskis, M. A. (1999). *History and educational policymaking*. New Haven, CT: Yale University Press.

Vogell, H. (2011, July 6). Investigation into APS cheating finds unethical behavior across every level. *The Atlanta Journal-Constitution*. Retrieved from www.ajc.com/news/investigation-into-aps-cheating-1001375.html

Wagner, T. (2008). *The global achievement gap: Why even our best schools don't teach the new survival skills our children need—and what we can do about it*. New York, NY: Basic Books.

Wagner, T. (2012). *Creating innovators: The making of young people who will change the world*. New York, NY: Scribner.

Watkins, C. L. (1995). Follow Through: Why didn't we. *Effective School Practices, 15*(1), 6.

Watkins, C. L. (1997). *Project Follow Through: A case study of contingencies influencing instructional practices of the educational establishment*. Cambridge, MA: Cambridge Center for Behavioral Studies.

Wentzel, K. R. (1991). Social competence at school: Relation between social responsibility and academic achievement. *Review of Educational Research, 61*(1), 1–24.

West-Knights, I. (2017, January 27). Why are schools in China looking west for lessons in creativity? *Financial Times*. Retrieved from www.ft.com/content/b215c486-e231-11e6-8405-9e5580d6e5fb

What Works Clearinghouse. (2014). *Procedures and standards handbook version 3.0*. Retrieved from ies.ed.gov/ncee/wwc/Docs/referenceresources/wwc_procedures_v3_0_standards_handbook.pdf

Whitney, A. K. (2016, January 27). The man who tried to kill math in America. *The Atlantic*. Retrieved from www.theatlantic.com/education/archive/2016/01/the-man-who-tried-to-kill-math-in-america/429231/

Willingham, A. (2017, May 24). How to make sense of the school choice debate. *CNN*. Retrieved from www.cnn.com/2017/05/24/us/school-choice-debate-betsy-devos/index.html

Witte, J. F. (2001). *The market approach to education: An analysis of America's first voucher program*. Princeton, NJ: Princeton University Press.

Wolf, P. J., Kisida, B., Gutmann, B., Puma, M., Eissa, N., & Rizzo, L. (2013). School vouchers and student outcomes: Experimental evidence from Washington, DC. *Journal of Policy Analysis and Management, 32*(2), 246–270.

Wraga, W. G. (2001). Left out: The villainization of progressive education in the United States. *Educational Researcher, 30*(7), 34–39.

Wu, H.-H. (2000). The 1997 mathematics standards war in California. In S. Stotsky (Ed.), *What's at stake in the K–12 standards wars: A primer for educational policy makers* (pp. 3–31). New York, NY: Peter Lang.

Wu, J. (2015, February 2). Guonei jingbansu jiazhang meinian jiating jiaoyu zhichu chao liu qiang yuan [Nearly half of Chinese families' education expenditure over 6,000 yuan]. Retrieved from www.thepaper.cn/newsDetail_forward_1300235

Yatvin, J. (2000). *Minority view.* Retrieved from www.nichd.nih.gov/publications/pubs/nrp/Documents/minorityView.pdf

Young, M. D. (1958). *The rise of the meritocracy, 1870–2033: An essay on education and equality.* London, UK: Thames & Hudson.

Zhao, Y. (2006). Creativity cannot be taught, but it can be killed. *Detroit Free Press.* Retrieved from www.freep.com/apps/pbcs.dll/article?AID=/20060116/OPINION02/601160310/1070/OPINION02&template=printart

Zhao, Y. (2009). *Catching up or leading the way: American education in the age of globalization.* Alexandria, VA: Association for Supervision and Curriculum Development.

Zhao, Y. (2012a). Flunking innovation and creativity. *Phi Delta Kappan, 94*(1), 56–61.

Zhao, Y. (2012b). *World class learners: Educating creative and entrepreneurial students.* Thousand Oaks, CA: Corwin.

Zhao, Y. (2014). *Who's afraid of the big bad dragon: Why China has the best (and worst) education system in the world.* San Francisco, CA: Jossey-Bass.

Zhao, Y. (2015a). *Lessons that matter: What we should learn from Asian school systems.* Retrieved from www.mitchellinstitute.org.au/reports/lessons-that-matter-what-should-we-learn-from-asias-school-systems/

Zhao, Y. (2015b). A world at risk: An imperative for a paradigm shift to cultivate 21st century learners. *Society, 52*(2), 129–135.

Zhao, Y. (Ed.). (2016a). *Counting what counts: Reframing education outcomes.* Bloomington, IN: Solution Tree Press.

Zhao, Y. (2016b). From deficiency to strength: Shifting the mindset about education inequality. *Journal of Social Issues, 72*(4), 716–735.

Zhao, Y. (2016c, November 29). It must be the chopsticks: The less reported findings of 2015 TIMSS and explaining the East Asian outstanding performance. Retrieved from zhaolearning.com/2016/11/29/it-must-be-chopsticks-the-less-reported-findings-of-2015-timss-and-explaining-the-east-asian-outstanding-performance/

Zhao, Y. (2016d). Numbers can lie: The meaning and limitations of test scores. In Y. Zhao (Ed.), *Counting what counts: Reframing education outcomes* (pp. 13–30). Bloomington, IN: Solution Tree Press.

Zhao, Y. (2016e, November 29). Stop copying others: TIMSS lessons for America. Retrieved from zhaolearning.com/2016/11/30/stop-copying-others-timss-lessons-for-america/

Zhao, Y. (2017, September). Fatal attraction: Why the West must stop copying China's flawed education system. *New Internationalist, 505*, 24–25.

Zhao, Y. (2018). *Reach for greatness: Personalizable education for all children.* Thousand Oaks, CA: Corwin.

Zhao, Y., & Wang, Y. (2018). Guarding the past or inventing the future: Education reforms in East Asia. In Y. Zhao & B. Gearin (Eds.), *Imagining the future of global education: Dreams and nightmares* (pp. 143–159). New York, NY: Routledge.

# Index

The letter *f* or *n* in a page reference refers to a figure or note, respectively.

# About the Author

*Yong Zhao* is a Foundation Distinguished Professor in the School of Education, with a courtesy appointment in the School of Business, at the University of Kansas. He is also a global chair in education at East China Normal University. He previously served as the presidential chair and director of the Institute for Global and Online Education in the College of Education, University of Oregon, where he was also a professor in the Department of Educational Measurement, Policy, and Leadership. Prior to Oregon, Yong Zhao was University Distinguished Professor at the College of Education, Michigan State University, where he also served as the founding director of the Center for Teaching and Technology and executive director of the Confucius Institute as well as the US-China Center for Research on Educational Excellence.

His works focus on the implications of globalization and technology on education. He has published over 100 articles and 30 books, including *Reach for Greatness: Personalizable Education for All Children* (Corwin, 2018), *Counting What Counts: Reframing Education Outcomes* (Solution Tree, 2016), *Never Send a Human to Do a Machine's Job: Correcting the Top 5 EdTech Mistakes* (Corwin, 2015), *Who's Afraid of the Big Bad Dragon: Why China Has the Best (and Worst) Education System in the World* (Jossey-Bass, 2014), *World Class Learners: Educating Creative and Entrepreneurial Students* (Corwin, 2012), and *Catching Up or Leading the Way: American Education in the Age of Globalization* (ASCD, 2009).